CRASH COURSE ON THE BIBLE

Crash Course on the Bible

Michael Gantt

Hodder & Stoughton
LONDON   SYDNEY   AUCKLAND

British Library Cataloguing in Publication Data
A record for this book is available from the British Library

ISBN 0 340 67865 8

Typeset by Palimpsest Book Production Limited,
Polmont, Stirlingshire
Printed and bound in Great Britain by
Cox & Wyman Ltd, Reading, Berkshire

Hodder and Stoughton Ltd
A division of Hodder Headline PLC
338 Euston Road
London NW1 3BH

To my father and mother

Acknowledgments

There are numerous people besides Merle and Phyllis Good and their fine company who have brought this book into being. If you find the book valuable, please join me in being grateful to them all. Without these people, this book simply would not be.

First, there are those who wrote the awe-inspiring books of the Bible.

Second, there are those who have preserved, studied, and taught, and – most of all – practised those books.

Third, there are those who, during my years of ministry, believed in me enough to support my own study, teaching, and stumbling practice of the Bible.

Fourth, there is Alan Kellock, my trusted literary agent and treasured friend, whose role in the publication of this book cannot be overstated.

Fifth, there is Joan Ziegler, my multitalented administrative assistant and esteemed co-worker, whose contributions to the writing of this book are too great to quantify.

Last, there is my faithful wife Janie and the four wonderful children – Jennifer, Jason, Jessica, and Jonathan – whom she has given me. Without them . . . well, I just can't imagine this book – or anything else – without them.

Michael Gantt

Contents

Introduction

Is it possible to read the Bible without going to church? People do it all the time. You can, too. The Bible is not a private manual for churchgoing people. It's a book for everyone. Though it's been banned, burned, and buried, it still lives and is healthier than ever. It's the bestseller of bestsellers, leading all other books in sales year after year.

People who love books love the Bible, for it has so many of the qualities found in good books: adventure, drama, romance, truth, inspiration, elegant speech, and more. Like all great books, it is thought-provoking. While it gives answers, it also raises questions. The questions stimulate our thinking and make us better people. If you love books – good and great books – you'll love the Bible.

One of the reasons for the Bible's popularity is the very fact that it is a book. Books are great friends. They entertain and enlighten; they comfort and advise. Yet they can confront and challenge, too. They're always ready to speak, and equally ready to be silent. Best of all, they're not touchy. You don't have to worry about saying the wrong thing and having them turn on you . . . or turn away from you. Dried ink doesn't move.

Therefore, when people want to know more about God, truth, love, right and wrong, they often turn to a nonthreatening friend – a book. And no single book has spoken about these subjects to more people, more compellingly, than this book we call the Bible.

What makes a book good or great is not so much that it answers all our questions, but that it raises questions we ought to be asking. It makes us think. And it makes us think better than we would without it. A good friend will likewise help us wrestle with our decisions but will not make them for us. If a good book is a good friend, then it's no mistake to call the Bible 'the Good Book'.

This book is intended as a guide to the Bible for people who don't know a lot about the Bible, but who may wish they knew more. Many people own a Bible but seldom read it, partly because they don't have anyone to help them understand it. My goal is to help nonchurchgoers understand the Bible better. Some churchgoers may look over our shoulders and find this introduction to the Bible helpful. That's fine with me. I don't wish to make a case against church attendance – merely recognise that people without an interest in church may still have an interest in the Bible.

Most of us – whether we go to church or not – would probably like to read the Bible more than we do. Why don't we? Often it's fear. At one extreme we're afraid we won't understand it and that we'll end up just wasting our time. At the other extreme we're afraid we will understand it and that we'll end up going religiously overboard. These fears can be overcome.

As for being afraid we won't understand, the only ability you need for reading the Bible is the ability to read. Parts of it are hard to understand, but all you have to do is learn how to skip those parts until they're not so hard any more. It used to be that the comics were the only part of the newspaper I understood. A few years later the sports section made sense. A few more years and I was able to read the whole thing. Except the commodities information on the financial page – I still don't understand how to read that. But not understanding every page has not kept me from reading and enjoying a newspaper. Likewise, you can read and enjoy the Bible as long as you can find parts that hold your interest and reward your attention. I'll help you find those parts.

As for being afraid we will understand . . . and become religious freaks, the Bible is the best safeguard against religious extremism. The more familiar you are with the Bible's contents, the more quickly you will recognise when someone is misquoting or misapplying it. A religious cult often arises when people mindlessly follow someone else's interpretation of life or the Bible. Reading the Bible for yourself will make you more able to develop and depend upon your own understanding of it. Yes, people differ about the Bible's meaning. But we also differ about love, freedom, responsibility, and everything else that's important. The fact the everyone doesn't see the Bible the same way is no reason to avoid it. It's all the more reason to read it for yourself.

No matter which English translation of the Bible you use, this guide will help you. Translations very in the small points, but they all convey the same major ideas. And though Bible scholars may debate whether Moses lived during the thirteenth or fifteenth centuries BC you don't need to enter that debate in order to read and understand what your Bible says about Moses. My approach will be to take the Bible at face value, just as every reader finds it. As with any book, you are always free to dispute any of its claims. But you can't accept or reject a book's claims until you know what those claims are. You can learn those claims better by reading the text itself than by wading through esoteric theories about the text. This guide, therefore, leads you away from scholarly debates and towards the Bible itself.

The eleven chapters of *Crash Course on the Bible* are organised into three distinct parts. The first part deals with the Bible as a whole. These three chapters describe how the Bible is similar to, and different from, any other book. The second part tackles the individual books of the Bible – from Genesis to Revelation. These seven chapters further prepare you to read with understanding any specific book of the Bible. The third and last part of the book will provide more pointers for exploring the Bible as a vast storehouse of literature and ideas.

Long before you finish this guide you'll start to have a better grasp of the Bible. From the beginning you'll see the obstacles that make reading the Bible difficult – and how to get round them. With each chapter you'll become more confident that you can indeed find your way around this perennial bestseller. And in the end, it will be your own opinion of the Bible that will matter to you most.

Crash Course on the Bible is a road map. It seeks to guide you through the twists and turns of the Bible countryside. Whether you've previously seen some of that countryside, or none of it, there is always more to be seen. I've been reading the Bible daily for close to two decades, and I'm still finding new and interesting vistas. If you'd like some help exploring the landscape, without detours for church issues or academic debates, this guide could be an answer to your prayer. If you're ready, fasten your seat belt and let's go!

Part One

The Whole of the Bible

The Structure of the Bible

If you can read a book, you can read the Bible. The very word 'Bible' comes from a word meaning 'book' or 'books'. That's what the Bible is: words on paper, glued and stitched, sitting between covers. The Bible is approachable by anyone who can approach a book. Further, if you like good books, you'll love 'the Good Book'. It's chock-full of all the things that make a book good. But there are some differences between the Bible and most other books. Failing to appreciate these differences can make your reading of the Bible confusing, frustrating, and dull; appreciating them makes the Bible more readable and enjoyable. The most important of these differences, and one of the first anyone who tries to read the Bible can notice, has to do with its size.

The Bible Is Big

The Bible is big. Very big. Some editions will easily dominate a coffee table. Other editions are small enough to be held in one hand . . . but then the print is so small that you have to hold a magnifying glass in your other hand. Therefore, the big display editions and the small compact editions – each in their own way – attest to the multitude of words in the Bible. Even the editions which are designed for comfortable reading – as opposed to exhibiting or carrying purposes – still must be printed on thin paper to keep the size of the book manageable. But while the Bible's bulk may be kept within the range of most books, its word count actually dwarfs them.

Just how big is the Bible? Stack ten average-sized nonfiction books printed today. That pile will contain the same number of words as are found in one Bible. Ten books! That's approaching one million words. And when you consider that most Bibles come with a number of words added – footnotes, verse numbers, and so on – the mass of words increases. All that thin Bible paper is concealing a mountain of material between its covers.

The first hurdle to overcome in reading the Bible, therefore, is its size. All other things being equal, most readers are not going to reach for a book that is weighed in pounds instead of ounces. If there are only two books to read, and one's short and the other's long, which one are most people going to reach for first? That's right. We'll read the long one later. That's another reason why even though the Bible is on most people's reading lists, it seldom comes to the top.

But there's a reason the Bible is so thick. And it's not because someone sat down with the idea of writing a long book about God. For if we dare to peel back the Bible's covers and look at the table of contents or flip through its pages, we see that the Bible is not a single writing. It's a collection of writings. This is not a mountain any more – it's a bunch of little hills. What looks insurmountable to read from a distance begins to look a lot more negotiable when you get up close.

The Bible Is a Collection of Many Pieces

The Bible appears to us as a book. And it is. But upon opening it, we see that it is a collection of books. Or at least a collection of writings. If you let it fall open to the middle, you will probably find yourself in the book of Psalms, which is itself a collection of 150 different pieces of writing. With this many different pieces of writing and hundreds upon hundreds of pages, the Bible begins to look less like a book and more like an encyclopaedia, or even a library.

An encyclopaedia, a library, and the Bible are all collections. An encyclopaedia is a collection of articles organised alphabetically by subject. A library is a collection of books organised by type of book and author. The Bible is a collection, too.

The 150 Psalms are each no longer than most encyclopaedia articles. Most of the rest of the Bible books are longer than encyclopaedia articles, but shorter than most of the books on any library bookshelf.

Some Bible books are as short as half a page. One of the longest books – Jeremiah – is roughly the length of today's short novel. This makes the Bible's longest book over a hundred times longer than its shortest book. This bunch of little hills is by no means uniform – they can vary drastically from each other in size. Regardless of the length, however, each of these pieces of the Bible is called a book.

We now see the reason for the Bible's massive size: it's not so much a book as a collection. No one person sat down and laboured to produce this huge volume. Instead, it is the accumulation of writings produced over centuries by many different authors. Individually, none of these books may be very long. But put them all together and you've got some bulk! No wonder the Bible's a big book – it's a bunch of little books glued together.

Instead of seeing the Bible as one of the longest books on a list of those we want to read, we should see it as a collection of the shortest. The Bible as a whole is much longer than any other book we'd like to read. But its individual books are mostly shorter than any other book we want to read. Therefore, when we're short on time, we can choose from the Bible's library because it contains so many different compact volumes. For while we usually go to a library to find a book, the Bible is a book that when we go to it, we find a library. The most we'd ever read of a library is a portion of its contents at any one time, and we ought to approach the Bible in the same way . . . lest we be overwhelmed!

Likewise, we wouldn't think of reading an encyclopaedia from cover to cover – it wasn't designed for that type of reading. It was designed that we might selectively use its different contents as we have interest. The Bible is best approached as we would an encyclopaedia – not reading from beginning to end, but going to a specific place from time to time.

The Bible's Pieces Can Be Very Different From Each Other

Except for their length, encyclopaedia articles look pretty much alike. Those who write them are contemporaries of each other. Rules of style are laid down by the publisher. The books of a library, however, show much more variety. A book on football may read quite differently from a book on philosophy. The authors are not trying to match styles. Besides, the philosophy book could have been written in the eighteenth century and the football book in the twentieth. For this reason, the bible is even more like a library than an encyclopaedia.

The books of the Bible have dozens of authors. These authors were often not contemporaries. Their lives were spread out over more than a thousand years. This situation does not produce the uniformity you see in an encyclopaedia, but the variety you see in a library. And the great variety is a matter of style as well as size.

You would expect a variety of styles if the authors wrote during different centuries. As many as sixteen centuries may have separated the author of the Bible's first book from the author of its last. Someone has said that the Bible was written not by one person, but by a committee. That may be, but it was a committee that never met. It's no wonder the Bible's pieces are so diverse.

The Bible's Pieces Are Organised

Even though the pieces of the Bible are often very different from each other, they're gathered and ordered to help the reader. A library is where writings are stored and organised so that readers may come and find them. As you enter a library, you discover that biographies are in one place, the remaining nonfiction in another, and so on. There's organisation and order. Librarians don't just pile all the books in a corner and tell the patrons to hunt. Likewise, the Bible comes arranged for us in a certain order. Once we understand the order in the library, we can pursue any area that interests us. The same is true with the Bible.

The 'rightness' of the order is not our concern. While all libraries are ordered, they're not all ordered the same way. Some Bibles are arranged differently from others, as I'll explain. It's not a matter of which arrangement is 'right'. There's more than one way to arrange the medicine cabinet in your home. Your goal is not to pass judgment on it, but to understand it. Otherwise, some dark night might find you taking an antacid when you need headache relief, or some sleepy morning brushing your teeth with ointment.

We're going to take a walking tour of the sections of the Bible just as if it were this library we've been talking about. Later, we'll spend a whole chapter on each of these sections, so don't labour over unfamiliar book titles. Focus rather on the 'library' and kinds of books that are in its various 'sections'. Our walk through the Bible books will reveal that the order in which they've been arranged is not random. As with a library, books of the same type have been put together. Each group of like books can be viewed as a section. And each section can be given a label.

Figures 1.1 and 1.2 display the various books as if they were on the shelves in a library. Remember that the Bible's largest book is over a hundred times the size of its smallest. So these books haven't been drawn to scale. These Figures, therefore, obscure the vast differences in the size of the respective books.

You may also want to open your Bible to its table of contents and check off the titles as we walk through. In all likelihood, the books in your Bible are arranged in precisely the order that I give here. If not, make note; at the end of the tour I'll show how to adjust for your particular Bible.

The Books of Moses

The first five books of the Bible – *Genesis, Exodus, Leviticus, Numbers*, and *Deuteronomy* – are traditionally assumed to

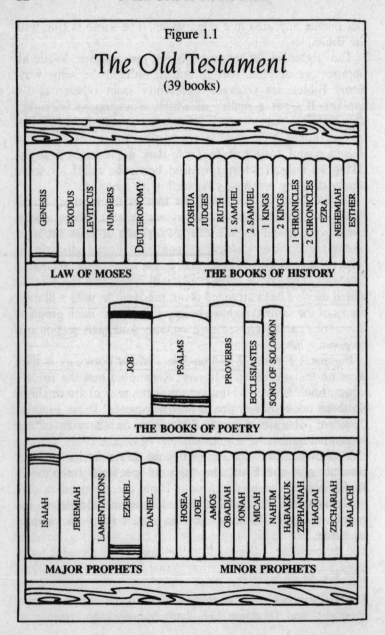

Figure 1.1

The Old Testament
(39 books)

GENESIS EXODUS LEVITICUS NUMBERS DEUTERONOMY

LAW OF MOSES

JOSHUA JUDGES RUTH 1 SAMUEL 2 SAMUEL 1 KINGS 2 KINGS 1 CHRONICLES 2 CHRONICLES EZRA NEHEMIAH ESTHER

THE BOOKS OF HISTORY

JOB PSALMS PROVERBS ECCLESIASTES SONG OF SOLOMON

THE BOOKS OF POETRY

ISAIAH JEREMIAH LAMENTATIONS EZEKIEL DANIEL

MAJOR PROPHETS

HOSEA JOEL AMOS OBADIAH JONAH MICAH NAHUM HABAKKUK ZEPHANIAH HAGGAI ZECHARIAH MALACHI

MINOR PROPHETS

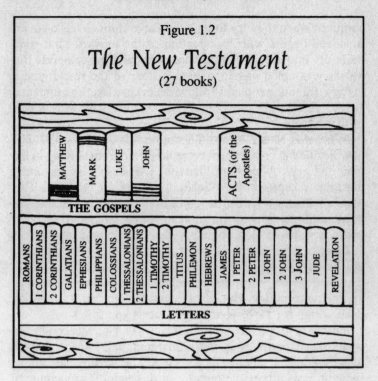

Figure 1.2

The New Testament
(27 books)

MATTHEW MARK LUKE JOHN ACTS (of the Apostles)

THE GOSPELS

ROMANS 1 CORINTHIANS 2 CORINTHIANS GALATIANS EPHESIANS PHILIPPIANS COLOSSIANS 1 THESSALONIANS 2 THESSALONIANS 1 TIMOTHY 2 TIMOTHY TITUS PHILEMON HEBREWS JAMES 1 PETER 2 PETER 1 JOHN 2 JOHN 3 JOHN JUDE REVELATION

LETTERS

come from Moses. For this reason they are sometimes called the books of Moses or the Law of Moses.

Before Moses there was no Bible. What he is usually credited with writing became the cornerstone of all the Bible writings that followed. Rare is the Bible that doesn't mention Moses or something he said. Even when he is not specifically mentioned, his ideas are present.

Genesis tells the story of the ancestors of Moses and his people. Central among these ancestors was a man named Abraham, and so his story – including facts about his ancestors and descendants – is central to this book. Some people today engage in genealogical research so that fellow family members might know their roots. Moses was doing the same for his fellow Israelites, who were several centuries removed from their ancestor Abraham. This explains why many people are confused when they try to read the Bible from cover to cover. It indeed begins with the creation of the universe, but soon trails off into specific family incidents and genealogies. But Moses was not trying to write a history of the world; just a history for his people. Worldwide events like creation and Noah's flood were mentioned only because they were a part of that history.

In *Exodus* Moses brings the story to his own time. He tells how he and his countrymen were delivered from slavery in the land of Egypt. A resistant Pharaoh, a series of plagues, and a dramatic escape through the Red Sea are all included. This book concludes with the Israelites in the wilderness at the foot of Mount Sinai. Moses was at the top of the mountain receiving instructions from God, including the Ten Commandments.

Leviticus has hardly any storytelling. It's a book of regulations for the Israelites concerning animal sacrifice, proper diet, and so on. Most folks find it as interesting to read as an insurance policy. But Jesus found the Golden Rule buried deep within it ('Love your neighbour as yourself').

Numbers gets its name from the census that was conducted while the nation was in the wilderness. They spent about a year building a tabernacle for God. This tabernacle can be thought of as a portable temple. In that time, it was common for each nation to have a temple for its primary god. This book also records that the Israelites' entrance into the promised land was delayed by forty years because of their disobedience.

Deuteronomy is the impassioned speech Moses gave as the forty-year wait was ending and just before he himself was to die. He exhorts the nation to remember all he has taught them. He emphasises that God was giving them a land of their own. It had long been promised to the descendants of Abraham. Hence, it was called the promised land. Only their faithfulness to God would allow the Israelites to remain on this land.

Books of History

While the first five books are usually attributed to Moses, the next twelve are attributed to no single author. They do, however, continue recording the history of the people of Israel. These twelve books of history cover roughly a thousand years.

The sixth book of the Bible is titled for Joshua, the man who took over leadership of Israel when Moses died. It tells of Israel's conquest of the promised land. After Israel settles the land, Joshua dies a natural death.

The next book is called *Judges* and picks up where *Joshua* left off. Israel's leaders who came after Moses and Joshua were called judges. They were not regarded as kings, but did lead Israel in battle against foreign oppressors. The little book of *Ruth,* which follows, tells the story of a special family who lived during the time of the Judges. The books of *1 Samuel, 2 Samuel, 1 Kings,* and *2 Kings,* which immediately follow *Judges* and *Ruth*, provide a four-volume history of the kings of Israel. The Israelites tired of God's system of judges and decided they wanted a king since each of the surrounding nations had one. There was a long line of kings, as there had been of judges. At the end of this period, Israel was defeated by Babylon and exiled from the land of promise.

1 Chronicles and *2 Chronicles* repeat the history of Israel's kings given in *1 & 2 Samuel and 1 & 2 Kings*. We thus have two accounts of Israel's kings, just as we have four accounts of Jesus's life (*Matthew, Mark, Luke*, and *John*). In each case it's the same story from a different perspective.

The last three history books are *Ezra, Nehemiah,* and *Esther*, which tell something of the times after Israel's exile from the land. While many Israelites became scattered throughout the world, a few of them returned to re-establish residence on the land promised to the descendants of Abraham. The glory of the nation had faded, but their hope for the future was still intact.

Books of Poetry

The first seventeen books of the Bible record history. When we come to the eighteenth, we see an abrupt change. In fact, the next five books make up a category all their own. They are called wisdom literature or books of poetry. We'll say more about the nature of this poetry later. For now, we'll keep to the quick tour.

First is *Job*. All the action is at the very beginning and the very end. Most of the book is dialogue. It reads like a script for a play. The subject? The sufferings of the righteous.

Psalms, as we said earlier, is composed of 150 different pieces. A psalm is like a song: some are sad, some are joyful, some are pensive, some are explosive.

Proverbs is a collection of . . . well, proverbs. There are over five hundred of them. Though written long ago, they deal wisely with human nature, which doesn't seem to have changed much over these thousands of years.

Ecclesiastes is yet another style of writing. It reads like an essay. It extols wisdom, but warns that achieving it will not answer all your questions.

The last book of this section is called *Song of Songs* and takes the form of a romantic love poem. Its colourful and sensual language can make you blush.

These five pieces of writing are so different from each other that they only look alike when you compare them with the books that precede them and follow them.

Books of Prophecy

The first twenty-two entries in the Bible are of Moses, of history, and of poetry. The remaining seventeen books of what is called the Old Testament are known as the books of prophecy. The first five are called the major prophets, and the next twelve are called the minor prophets. The major and minor distinction doesn't refer to the prophets themselves, but to the relative length of their writings. The writings of the first group are generally longer than the writings of the second.

Isaiah spoke and wrote a century or so before the end of the Israelite kingdom and Israel's exile from the land. *Jeremiah* himself lived through that terrible time. *Lamentations* is his elegy over the destruction of his homeland. *Ezekiel* is one of those Israelites who was taken captive into the land of Babylon.

Daniel, also, was taken away from the land of Israel and spoke for God on foreign soil.

The remaining twelve prophets (the minor prophets) – *Hosea, Joel, Amos, Obadiah, Jonah, Micah, Nahum, Habakkuk, Zephaniah, Haggai, Zechariah,* and *Malachi* – may have written shorter pieces, but they were just as zealous in their denunciation of evil and just as sure of their hope in God.

The first nine of the minor prophets were roughly contemporary with the time from Isaiah to Jeremiah. The last three lived after the return from exile.

If we include the books of Moses (which give history as well as laws) with the books of history, we can divide the thirty-nine books of the Old Testament into the following three groups:

History – 17
Poetry – 5
Prophecy – 17

Therefore, perusing the books of the Bible reveals not only certain natural groupings, but a memorable proportioning.

Most of Israel's history is found in the first seventeen books. The books of poetry and prophecy do give some historical details. But those details fit within the time frame laid down by the first seventeen books. History picks up again with the four gospels in the New Testament.

The Four Gospels

Matthew, Mark, Luke and *John* are some of the best known writers of Bible books. Almost everyone has heard their names and knows that they wrote about the life of Jesus. Each of these four books is called a 'gospel', meaning 'good news' and referring to Jesus – His life, death, and resurrection. Each Gospel provides a different perspective on Jesus's ministry and message.

Like the historical records of the earlier books of the Bible, the Gospels mainly tell of words spoken and deeds done. The elegant descriptions of scenery and elaborate descriptions of motive and interior dialogue that we are used to in modern writing are largely absent. The Bible's narratives don't so much tug at you to turn the pages as they dig in their heels to make you stop and think.

The Book of Acts

All four Gospels end with Jesus's resurrection from the dead on the third day after He was crucified. The book of *Acts* picks up at this point and records Jesus's ascension into heaven forty days after the resurrection. For the rest of the book, Jesus is regarded as active in heaven while the disciples are dominating the earthly scene. The pupils have become teachers. The full name for the book is the *Acts of the Apostles*.

With the end of the book of *Acts* comes the end of the history of the Bible. Oh, certain other things can be deduced from the letters that follow. But those details conform to the history laid down by the Gospels and *Acts* in the same way that the books of poetry and prophecy conform to the time frame laid down by the books of history that preceded them.

The Apostles' Letters

The remaining books of the Bible are all letters, or epistles, as they are sometimes called. They were written in the early days of the Church – before it became an institution. It was a movement then . . . a movement of people who believed that this Jewish Messiah named Jesus had indeed been raised from the dead and was reigning in heaven.

It is traditionally assumed that most of the letters were written by a disciple named Paul (specifically, *Romans, 1 & 2 Corinthians, Galatians, Ephesians, Philippians, Colossians, 1 & 2 Thessalonians, 1 & 2 Timothy, Titus,* and *Philemon*). Unlike all the other letters, *Hebrews* does not identify its author. There was a single letter from James (*James*). Then a handful from Peter (*1 & 2 Peter*) and John (*1, 2 & 3 John*). Finally, the Bible ends with a little letter from Jude (*Jude*) and a blockbuster from John (*Revelation* – also called the Apocalypse).

Taking Stock

We'll have more to say about every one of these Bible books later. In the second part of this guide there's a chapter for each section. But for now we've completed our brief walking tour of the Bible library. Please notice that we have not rearranged any of the Bible books. We have taken them in the order we found them and noticed that they have been gathered and ordered. Another way to understand the structure of the Bible is to view it like a deck of playing cards (the numbers aren't too far apart – fifty-two compared to sixty-six). When you're dealt a hand in a game of cards, the first thing you usually do is arrange your hand. How you arrange it depends on the game you're playing. Generally, you arrange them according to suit (all spades together, all hearts, and so on). Then you arrange the cards within each suit. Perhaps ascending order or maybe descending.

You might not arrange the cards in your hand the same way as someone else at the table. You may even vary your own style from time to time. The essential thing is not *which* order, but that there's order. And the purpose of order is to know what you're holding and to be able to find each card when you need it. The cards in your Bible deck have been arranged in a certain order. First, by suit. That is, history, poetry, and so on. Then within each suit by some other order. For example, chronologically in the case of the history books.

You or I might have arranged the Bible books differently. We might have put prophecy books before the poetry books. Or we might have ordered them all alphabetically by title. Wives don't always order the bookshelves the same way as their husbands – even when they read the same books. Our goal is not to critique the order. It's glued in place anyway. We just want to understand it so we can put our hands on the book we want.

That's why, even if the books in your Bible are ordered

differently from mine, you can still find your way around. Though your order may be different, there's still an order that can be found.

What If Your Bible Doesn't Match This List?

Does your Bible have fewer books than I have listed? It is probably a Jewish Bible. A modern-day Jewish Bible won't have the four Gospels, *Acts*, and the apostles' letters (what is collectively called the New Testament). It might also show the books it does have in a different order and with different names from those I have listed. For example, *1 Chronicles* and *2 Chronicles* may be combined and called simply *Chronicles*. And often the twelve minor prophets are combined as one book. Given these kinds of combinations, some Jewish Bibles have as few as twenty-two books, but the material would be the same as the thirty-nine books I have listed from Moses to *Malachi*. And whatever the order and combination of the books in your Bible, it's still Moses' books you'll find at the beginning, for, as we said, his five books are the foundation of the Bible – no matter what version you have. Even though your Bible may be shorter than the one I have described, you will still be able to find help from this guide. So follow along, making adjustments as they seem appropriate to you.

If your Bible has more books than I've listed, you probably have an Eastern Orthodox or Roman Catholic Bible. Some Protestant groups have a longer Bible, too. The additional books would be in the Old Testament, for the twenty-seven books of the New Testament are undisputed in our day. All Bibles with a New Testament have these twenty-seven no more, no less.

The extra books are in the Old Testament and are often called the Apocrypha (not to be confused with Apocalypse which, as we saw earlier, is another name for the book of *Revelation*). The number of books involved varies: Roman Catholics include more than Protestants; Eastern Orthodox more than Roman Catholics. In either case, it is not a great deal of material. In your Bible these books may sit in their own special section between the Old and New Testaments. Or your Bible may have them mixed within the Old Testament books. They were written after the prophets, but before the time of Jesus. Their presence or absence doesn't alter the meaning of the Bible.

As with those whose Bibles are shorter, you who have a longer one should still be able to follow along with the discussion and profit accordingly. Though the type of order may vary, the fact of order remains. And that is something all Bibles have in common.

Your Bible, however, is probably neither shorter nor longer than the one I'm using. It probably includes the exact books I have listed in exactly the order I've mentioned them. This sixty-six book Bible is the most common in circulation today.

'Sixty-Six Plus' Pieces of Writing in the Bible

We have found the Bible to be a very big book. And we have discovered that the reason for its size is that it's not just a book, but a collection of books. We've also seen that there's a tremendous variety, not just in the size of these books, but in their form and style. We've seen that the books are gathered and ordered in a thoughtful way. We've identified at least sixty-six distinct writings in the Bible. I say 'at least' because we've also noted that the single book of Psalms is easily divided into 150 particular pieces of writing. And then when you consider that over five hundred different proverbs make up the book of Proverbs, we have a very large number of distinct pieces in the Bible, some of them quite small.

We no longer have to be intimidated by the size of the Bible. It's not a big book, but a bunch of little books. When you go to the library for a book, you don't feel guilty that you're not reading all the other books in the library. Maybe you'll get to some of them; maybe you won't. You're just happy you have a book to read and happy there are more waiting for you when you want them. This is the attraction the Bible holds for those who understand its structure. The size that used to intimidate, now tends to invite. Within its covers we can always find something interesting enough and short enough to read.

The Bible is a buffet, able to satisfy all kinds of appetites. You can go to it again and again as you discover the types of food you really enjoy. There'll be times you experiment. Some experiments will turn out better than others. But the more often you return, the more you know those dishes that always seem to satisfy. People whose only experience with the Bible was trying to read it from beginning to end do not think much of it. They are like the fellow that starts at the beginning of the buffet, filling his plate. By the time he gets to the really good stuff, he has no room because his plate is loaded with salad and olives. He goes away feeling this restaurant is much overrated. But generations of satisfied diners know better.

I don't want to seem as if I'm opposed to the idea of reading the Bible from beginning to end. There may be times when you want to do this, and you'll be glad you did. But since the Bible was established in the very beginning as a collection or anthology (remember, Moses is credited with writing five books), why should we expect it to hold our interest indefinitely, as if it were written as a novel? Novelists, especially those who write longer books, know that a reader's interest must continually be aroused. The Bible doesn't usually sustain this kind of interest page after page, because it wasn't designed to.

There's nothing wrong with calling the Bible 'the Good Book'. But it would be even more descriptive and helpful to call it 'the Good Anthology'. Those who enjoy reading it approach it on that basis. Though 'the Good Anthology' doesn't have enough zip to ever catch on, try to remember it, and the Bible will become more accessible to you.

As you become increasingly familiar with the different sections of the Bible, you'll find yourself going to it more often and more comfortably. This reminds me of the boxes of chocolate I encountered as a child. I learned that there was a map in the lid that described each type of chocolate and its location in the box. Each one looked pretty much the same from the outside. But the insides were a different story. There was one kind that tasted like mud, and I wanted to be sure to avoid it. I learned it was called toffee. The lid told me the section to stay away from. When I got older, toffee became my favourite. My tastes changed, but I never wanted to be without that lid.

Finally, consider the structure and content of a newspaper. It doesn't just bring us a few major facts, like only about earthquakes. It brings us a multitude of facts, large and small, many of which we simply cannot digest at one time. When I tell my wife that I'm finished with the paper, she doesn't think that I've taken in all that it says. Even in my most thorough reading I won't have studied the classifieds, the retail ads, or the food section. Even people who own stocks and shares usually only read the lines on the financial pages that give the price of the stock they own (or wish they owned!). Likewise, the Bible contains much more information than just headlines.

There's a lot in the Bible we can skim. But as with the newspaper, the section we pass over at one stage in our lives may be the one we hurry to in others. When I was young, I bypassed everything for the cartoons. Things change. This is why it's impossible to identify which parts of the Bible are important and which parts can be skipped. Has this conversation ever happened at your house?

'The dog tore up parts of the paper,' he said.

'The important parts?' she asked.

'Depends. Let me show you the unchewed parts and see if you look relieved or depressed.'

What's important is what interests you. And what interests you now may or may not interest you ten years from now. No one can tell you what the important parts of the Bible are. You have to get in and find out for yourself.

The most important thing to remember from this chapter is that the Bible is much easier to read if you approach it as a collection of books rather than as a single book. If the only way you were allowed to read your big Sunday newspaper was word for word from page one to the end, you'd probably put off reading it as much as you put off reading the Bible. It's your understanding about how the paper is organised that allows you to go to the sections that interest you. The more comfortable you become with the Bible's organisation, the more often you'll go to it and find pleasure reading it.

But understanding the Bible's structure as a bundle of books is only one of the things that makes it easier to read. There's another fact that opens the Bible to us. Bananas don't just come in a bunch – they come with skins. Once you pick the one you like, you'll still want to peel it before you take a bite. Let me explain.

2

Things Added to the Bible

Bananas grow in bunches. They can be taken from the tree and delivered to your table just that way. You see the particular banana you want. You pick it off. You pull back the skin and take a bite. Though you don't eat the skin, you're thankful for the purpose it's fulfilled. It has preserved and protected that banana you're munching.

The last chapter showed that the Bible is a bunch of books. This chapter will show that each Bible book comes to us in packaging, or in a skin. That is, there are elements present that were not part of what the original writers wrote. These elements were added by others to help us understand what was written. But we need to know that they were added, or else they'll deprive us of understanding. I'll show you what I mean.

Chapter and Verse Divisions

The chapter and verse divisions in our Bibles were not written by the Bible authors. They were added many years later. It's important that we don't assume, for example, that Matthew wrote a first chapter, then proceeded to a second, and so on. It might cause us to divide his thoughts in a way he didn't intend. And it will certainly make his work harder to read.

Chapter divisions in books written today are the author's doing. They help in ordering the thought. Chapters are to a book what sentences are to a paragraph. They break up the writer's thoughts into digestible pieces. For this reason, the writer controls where the chapters are divided, just as she or he controls where the full stops are placed.

But the chapter divisions in the Bible were not determined by those who wrote the words we read in the Bible. Chapter divisions were added to the text hundreds of years after the words were written and the authors had died. The original writers neither planned these divisions nor anticipated them. But we are so used to seeing Bibles with chapter and verse numbers that we can sometimes forget how unnatural they are. The chapter and verse numbers in the apostles' letters, for example, ought to appear as strange to us as the following:

> Dear Aunt Sue,
> Chapter One
> 1   Last week we went to town and
> 2   learned that . . .

Perhaps your correspondence will one day be so treasured that a numbering system will be applied to help people study it. But that won't mean you wrote it that way.

It's not that the chapter and verse divisions are bad. They help us find our way around in the Bible. For example, I mentioned earlier that Jesus found the Golden Rule in the depths of Leviticus. If you wanted to locate that passage, would you want to go looking for it armed with no more direction than that? Hardly. But if I wrote Leviticus 19:18, you'd know exactly the spot to turn to. First, you'd find the nineteenth chapter of Leviticus. Then you'd proceed down to the eighteenth verse of that chapter. There you'd find the words, 'Love your neighbour as yourself'.

The chapter and verse numbering system is as helpful as the latitude and longitude lines on a globe, which enable us to locate any point on the earth. The Grand Canyon, for example, is located at a point near 36 degrees latitude and 112 degrees longitude. But if you should make it to the Grand Canyon, you won't waste time asking the tour guide, 'Where are the lines?' You know they are imaginary.

The chapters and verses in the Bible should be regarded in the same way. They are not to be considered as part of the terrain.

When we learn to read a globe, we learn the proper use of the lines that crisscross it. Learning to read the Bible means learning to read the chapter and verse numbers in much the same way. All those lines are indispensable for locating things, but shouldn't be confused with the landscape. First came the earth; later, the latitude and longitude lines. First came the Bible books; later, the chapter and verse divisions. We should learn to read past the chapter and verse divisions, just as we look past the lines on the globe.

Some Bibles even go so far as to show paragraph markings within each chapter. One could argue that the writers wrote logically, and so these added divisions are following the contours of their thought. This is a good point because the Bible's style often seems to be a stringing together of paragraph-like segments. Thus, dividing it into paragraphs fits better than dividing it into chapters and verses. But we must remember that all these divisions are guesses, even if educated ones. The Bible's writers did not indent the paragraphs, number the sentences, or divide the chapters.

One place that the chapter divisions do fit nicely are the *Psalms*. Each psalm makes up its own chapter, and so there is a correspondence between the divisions of the chapters and the divisions of the thought. But this is one of the few places in the Bible where this is so. Right next door in *Proverbs*, the chapter divisions can be very misleading. Some of the proverbs are one or two lines, but others are longer. *Proverbs'* thirty-one chapters give the impression that there are thirty-one neat divisions. Reading the book, however, you see that it's not so neat. But then, the superimposed grid on the globe is neater and straighter than the reality of the earth. Though national boundaries may occasionally coincide with those lines, it's more often that they don't.

Printing and Binding

Another helpful addition to the Bible that needs to be properly understood, lest it confuse us, is its printing and binding. If you print sixty-six books in the same type, design them identically, and glue them together, you give the impression of a uniformity that the original texts did not have. In my English Literature class at school we were issued a very big textbook. It was an anthology containing a wide variety of the most important examples of good English writing. There were poems and short stories. Some pieces were humorous and some tragic. One page would hold adventure and the next page meditation. Not only did these books not read smoothly from beginning to end, they often didn't read smoothly from page to page. But they weren't designed to read smoothly. They were designed as a buffet. And while you may be eating food that is all served from the same table, you don't eat salad with a spoon or soup with a fork. As the nature of the food dictates the way it should be eaten, so the nature of the writing suggests the way it should be read.

The uniformity of Bible printing, however, sometimes obscures the variety in the Bible writings. Yet some of the variety still comes through. For example, we can tell from the arrangement of the lines on the page that the *Psalms* are to be read differently from the regulations in *Leviticus*. Poetry looks different from prose. But there are many Bibles in which the print style is the same for the laws in *Deuteronomy* as it is for the personal letter to *Philemon*. And the literary style of a letter from a good friend is going to be different from the literary style of a letter from the Inland Revenue.

This is not a complaint against Bible printers. If they start laying out the print in all the different styles required, we might need a wheelbarrow to move a Bible from the living room to the bedroom. Most of those styles would be judgment calls anyway. The solution is to read and let the material take its own shape in your mind. Don't let the fact that the text is laid out in exactly the same way from page to page lead you to assume that it can all be read at the same pace. Keep remembering that this is a collection of different books by different authors writing in different styles.

Another example of added uniformity is the matter of book titles. Most Bible books were not given titles by their authors. As with the chapter and verse divisions, titling came later for the purpose of identification. Each book had to have a name in order to be able to distinguish it from the others.

Some titles come from the subject matter (*Genesis, Exodus*). Some come from the name of the one who did the writing (*Isaiah, Jeremiah*), while some come from the name of the ones written to (*Romans, Ephesians*). The titles were determined by those who treasured the writings, not those who wrote them. It's obvious James didn't title his letter 'James', for you wouldn't title your letters 'George' or 'Helen', even if that was your name. All of which brings us to an interesting point.

Things Missing from the Bible

Some things that we're used to seem to be missing. For example:

* The Bible books are not missing titles, but they are missing *the kind of titles we are used to seeing* in a nonfiction book. The book titles we are accustomed to are creations of their authors and seek to encapsulate the messages of the books. For example, a title like *How to Fly a Kite* tells you the subject matter of the book. If there's any doubt, subtitles are often added. Bible book titles, on the other hand, don't do as much work. They're not irrelevant, but a single word with the occasional addition of a number (*1 Chronicles*) hardly carries the information we're used to in titles. Besides that, most titles of the Bible's books were applied by a reader because the original writing was untitled. Therefore, the kinds of titles we're used to are missing.

* The Bible books are not missing chapters, but they are missing them *in the way we are used to seeing them*. We are used to chapter divisions which serve to accomplish the

purpose of the book – each one a well-defined step, keeping us right in line with the writer's thoughts. As we've seen, the Bible's chapter divisions only help us to locate places in the book. The author was not around when the matter was decided. Therefore, we are missing the kind of chapters we are used to.

• There is a table of contents for the Bible as a whole, but none of the individual books have one. This, too, we are not used to being without. Most books have a table of contents in which the author lays out the course to be followed. Bible authors don't provide such a road map. Therefore, we are missing the kind of table of contents we are accustomed to.

• Since copyright laws didn't exist in Bible times, we do not have the kind of dating we expect in a book. We are used to flipping to the opening pages of a book to discover when the author produced the work, or at least when it was first published. It's hard to imagine a book with a missing copyright page. Archaeologists, historians, and Bible scholars can estimate dates for various writings, but they don't always agree, and their estimates can change with new discoveries. Therefore, the kind of dating we are used to associating with books is missing.

The book publishing industry as we know it today did not exist in those ancient times. If it had, these 'missing' things would probably have been provided. But they just weren't necessary then. It's like roads and road signs. The ancients had roads just as we still do today. But our roads have many more signs than theirs. We're whizzing so fast and winding so far that we'd be lost without them. 'Give way . . . Level crossing . . . 60 miles per hour . . .' But such signs would only clutter an ancient landscape. There were no level crossings, and you certainly couldn't exceed sixty miles an hour on a donkey. Ancient literature was less frantic than ours, just as their traffic was less frantic.

As you read the Bible more, you'll become less concerned

with the absence of catchy titles, tables of contents, meaningful chapter divisions, and dates of original publication. The road can be travelled without the extra signs we've grown accustomed to. Its gentle windings can be followed easily. You may even find yourself refreshed by the leisurely pace of an ancient road. The more you travel these roads, the more you'll see what I mean.

Notes

In addition to book titles and chapter and verse numbering, our Bibles usually come packaged with a set of notes. These, too, are the added work of those who've studied the Bible and not that of the Bible authors themselves.

We're used to seeing footnotes in some books. But in a Bible they may not only appear along the bottom; they might be on the side or in the middle. There are a number of different ways to organise the notes, and each Bible usually gives its own explanation. Many of us are wary of books filled with footnotes. They remind us too much of school. But you can train your eye to read past the notes, just the way you read past the chapter and verse divisions.

As we've said, these notes were not produced by the authors. Then why are they there? Usually it has something to do with the way a word or phrase was translated. Unless your Bible has the Old Testament books printed in Hebrew and the New Testament books printed in Greek, it's a translation. Most people in the world today do not speak either of these two languages, and so most of the Bibles printed are translations.

Translation

Technically, translation may not be something that's added to the Bible. But it's a process our Bibles had to go through before they got to us. Translating is not easy work. Even the brightest scholars don't always agree about how to translate every single word or sentence. When there's uncertainty, they'll often include a footnote explaining other possible translations. Or maybe they're sure of the translation but want to offer a further explanation that makes the meaning clearer. For example, the word translated could be 'Gentile'. A note might be added explaining what this word means: anyone who is not a Jew. Such a note clarifies the translation.

Bible scholars are very respectful of the writing in the Bible. They want to pass it on to us in its purest form. That means adding notes in such a way that the text itself looks as much as possible like the original writer intended. The text is what the Bible author wrote, and the notes below or beside are what was added. Bible writers never produced their own footnotes because they wrote in the language of their readers and listeners. Notes on translation weren't necessary for them.

Concerning translation, some people argue about which is 'best' or 'right'. Most of us won't care about such arguments. It's fair to say that probably all translations are good, though none is perfect. Surely there are some interpreters at the United Nations who are better than others. And even with the good ones, we might not understand every single word. But as long as we're getting the gist of the message, we're satisfied.

If you're satisfied with the Bible you have, fine. There may be a few lines that seem unusual, but then there are some things your brother-in-law says that you don't quite follow either. If you think your translation could be improved on, head to the bookshop and see what they have. The more you read the Bible, the more you'll know what you want in a translation. Each translation usually states in a preface what it was intending to do.

Some translators strive for equivalent words ('You anoint my head with oil'), while other translators think it's better to use an equivalent idiom ('You welcome me as your guest'). Then some translators use a smaller vocabulary to make the translation readable to younger people. There are all sorts of ways to slice the pie. And language is always changing, so there's always room for a new translation. Some people will reach for the new, while others happily cling to the old, most notably the King James Version. Like many people, you may end up keeping more than one version because each has its own particular appeal to you.

Cross-References

When the Bible pages look really crowded, it's probably because cross-references have been included with the notes. Cross-references relate one passage of the Bible to others of similar thought or expression. For example:

In John 3:14 Jesus speaks of Himself as the Son of Man and says:

> Just as Moses lifted up the snake in the desert, so the
> Son of Man must be lifted up.

If your Bible has cross-references there will be a little superscript number or letter somewhere near the word 'Moses' or 'snake'. Then you find the corresponding entry in the notes on that page. At that place you will probably see something like:

Nu 21:9

This refers to the ninth verse of the twenty-first chapter of the book of Numbers. If you turn to that passage, you'll find the incident to which Jesus refers. It tells of Moses lifting up a bronze snake in the wilderness. Jesus's hearers, being Jews well-versed in their own history, knew of the incident to which Jesus was alluding. We who read the Bible thousands of years later, and who may not be familiar with Israelite history, are helped along by such a cross-reference.

Not all cross-references are so specific and direct. For example, 1 Corinthians 13:13 contains the line:

> And now these three remain: faith, hope and love.
> But the greatest of these is love.

The cross-reference here might be to any verse which contains a similar idea, such as 1 John 4:16 which says:

. . . God is love . . .

Not all cross-reference systems are identical. But you get the idea, which is to show the linkage of ideas throughout the various writings of the Bible. Some systems are so elaborate that the words of the Bible look surrounded and imprisoned by this mass of tiny print that can strain even the best eyes. For people who disdain footnoted books as being too academic, this is a veritable nightmare. But there are two easy solutions. You can buy a Bible without cross-references, whose pages are cleaner. Or you can train yourself to read past all the fine print.

The second solution may be best since you never know when you might want to take a side excursion to see what other Bible writers had to say about the same ideas. In doing that, you will discover what is one of the most amazing things about the Bible. That is, its unity.

Up to now I have hammered you incessantly with the Bible's variety and lack of uniformity. So what's this about unity? The unity is not found in form or style, but in its ideas. What Moses said, Isaiah believed. What Moses and Isaiah said, Jesus believed. What Moses and Isaiah and Jesus said, Peter believed. What Moses and Isaiah and Jesus and Peter said, Jude believed. Although each piece of writing can be read independently, its thinking has been built upon what was written before.

Using the cross-references is not the only way to see the unity of the Bible. It becomes apparent as you read the books themselves. In the middle of all that variety . . . unity. It mirrors the human race itself. In the midst of all our variety, there are things common to us all. Regardless of our skin colour, gender, or one of a hundred other things that may distinguish us, there is the equality of human life which unites us. And the unity of the Bible writers goes even beyond this, for they saw God and life with the same attitude.

The more you read the Bible, the more you'll wonder at how authors so diverse in personality, separated by so many years, can see things so similarly. It is like the wonder you sometimes see in a marriage where a husband and wife of wildly different temperaments still see the world the same way and seem to speak with the same voice. Like an orchestra with instruments as different as a piccolo and a tuba making one joyful expression of music, the Bible writers blend in an indescribable way. In fact, I'll say no more about it here. Like the beauty of a sunrise, it will overwhelm you when you see it, and you'll consider any prior description as being inadequate.

Other Things Added to the Bible

There is really no end of things that can be added to a Bible. I won't try to cover them all. So far I've mentioned those things that are found in almost every edition. Here are some that are only slightly less common.

Concordance. This is an alphabetical index often found in the back of a Bible. It lists words, the book (including chapter and verse) where they may be found, and at least a few of the words before and after to give the context. Here's what an entry might look like:

LOVE
　　　　Lev 19:18 1. your neighbour as yourself
　　　　Lk 6:27 1. your enemies
　　　　1 Co 13:13 the greatest of these is 1.
　　　　1 Jn 4:16 God is 1.

Any concordance in a Bible is selective. But there are concordances published separately which list every word and every place it occurs in the Bible. Needless to say, they're heavy.

Red Letters. Around AD 1900 someone got the idea of printing the words spoken by Jesus in red. It's as if the printer took a highlighter and marked just those words. It has become a popular feature.

Maps. No Bible writer ever drew a map – at least not one that managed to get preserved. Maps are drawn from facts discovered through historical and archaeological research.

There's usually more than one map in a Bible because boundaries and location names change over time. Think how much maps of your country have changed over the last three hundred years. Bible history covers a time period five times that long! The maps are usually labelled so you know which Bible books to associate with which map.

Special Marking for Old Testament Quotes. Most of the New Testament books quote directly from the Old Testament books. Many Bibles display these quotations with more than just quote marks to make them more recognisable. They may be printed in capitals or italics. Sometimes they're set apart from the rest of the text. For example, Paul (whose writings are in the New Testament) might quote Moses (whose writings are in the Old Testament) in this way (this is taken from 1 Corinthians 9:9–10):

> For it is written in the Law of Moses: 'DO NOT MUZZLE AN OX WHILE IT IS TREADING OUT THE GRAIN.' Is it about oxen that God is concerned? Surely he says this for us, doesn't he? Yes, this was written for us . . .

The translators are alerting the reader by means of the capital letters that Paul is quoting an Old Testament passage. If your Bible has a cross-reference system, it probably tells you the location of that verse. Paul himself didn't give it because, as we've said, chapter and verse numbers came long after the Bible was completed.

You might say, and you'd be right, that special marking wasn't necessary since Paul clearly stated he was quoting Moses. But many times such a preface isn't given. In those cases the writer omitted it because the readers or hearers would have recognised the quote without it, just as we'd recognise 'I have a dream . . .' without anyone specifically mentioning Martin Luther King. The translators are trying to help us with our lack of familiarity with the Bible. And even in cases where someone like Paul specifically states the source of the quotation, the translators still mark it off for the sake of consistency.

Introductions and Outlines. Some Bibles include an introduction to each book of the Bible written by Bible scholars. Such introductions contain the name of the author who wrote the Bible book, the approximate date it was written, and an explanation of its contents. In some cases, even an outline of the contents is given. You may recognise that the purpose behind all this is to give us the 'signs' we usually look to before beginning to read something. These may be helpful but can also be confusing. Bible scholars don't always agree on authorship and dating issues. One Bible may differ from another on such points. Underlying it all is the fact that these items have been added long after the author's death. Since the authors did not provide all these 'signs', we can only put so much faith in them.

Articles. Articles on various subjects can be added to Bibles. Some explain the culture of Bible times. Some explain how Bible history meshes with other historical records. Some explain theological positions. The subjects are endless.

Lists. Just as a concordance shows chapters and verses where certain words may be found, lists can be assembled showing chapters and verses for various subjects. For example, there could be a list of prayers found in the Bible. Or a list of miracles. Or a list of Israel's kings. As the possible articles are endless, so the possible lists are endless.

And Even More Things Added to the Bible

Beyond what we've mentioned, there are even more additions that people have made for the purpose of making the Bible easier to understand. As long as people read and study the Bible, new things will be added for the sake of understanding.

Speaking of study, some Bibles are actually called study Bibles. They include many more notes and cross-references than are normal. They also provide introductions and outlines for each book. A study Bible is usually assembled with a particular type of reader in mind. That is, it may be designed for teenagers, theological students, or all those of a particular theological or denominational persuasion.

Suffice it to say that you can sometimes pile so much help into the Bible that it becomes hard to find the Bible any more. Sometimes all the helps just need to be laid aside while the text speaks for itself. There's nothing wrong with listening to the commentary after a political speech, but if you want to form your own opinion, it's probably a good idea not to skip the speech itself. If the Bible writings are allowed to speak for themselves, they can say plenty. Psalm 23 has warmed a lot of hearts with never a mention of its original publication date.

Distinguishing the Bible from What's Been Added to It

The point of this chapter has been to draw a line between the Bible writings and the container they come in. We appreciate the packaging and labelling, but we don't want to confuse it with the contents. Otherwise we bite into a tasteless skin, and the delectable banana squishes out the sides. The drawn line isn't always easy to see, but at least you know it's there. Maybe now's the time to point out that even the terms 'Old Testament', 'New Testament', and 'Bible' are labels that came long after the Bible writings themselves.

It's not as though Isaiah thought to himself, 'I think God wants me to write a volume for the prophecy section of the Old Testament of the Bible.' He simply wrote. His fellow Israelites preserved and treasured the writing. When Jesus came along He spoke of it with the same reverence accorded to Moses' writing.

And it's not as though Paul thought to himself, 'I believe that I should write a book to be included in the New Testament of the Bible and a good title would be "*Galatians*".' It's obvious when you read Galatians that Paul was writing a letter to his followers in a region called Galatia. There was a problem in their understanding and he was trying to solve it. It was nothing like submitting a manuscript to be included in something called the Bible, much less the New Testament portion of it.

The word 'Bible' is not even in the Bible. That term came long after all the writings were completed and assembled. While the collection was still growing, writers would refer to the then existing collection by various terms, but never 'Bible'. The earliest terms made some reference to Moses because he probably wrote the first books: 'The law of Moses', 'The law of the Lord', or simply 'Moses'. Since the additional writings were considered the work of prophets, the common term came to be 'Moses and the Prophets' or something similar. By New Testament times, another common term was 'Scripture' or 'the Scriptures'. Figure 2.1 displays the variety of terms used in the Bible to refer to the Bible.

The simplest generic term for the collection was *writings*, often with the adjective 'sacred' or 'holy' added. Whenever you come across these various terms in your Bible reading, it will reinforce the idea that the Bible was not written as a single book. That someone has bound these writings together and delivered them to us is wonderful, but we shouldn't confuse the bundle with the writings they contain. Just as 'Bible' is a term that has come to be applied to this collection of writings, so also the terms 'Old Testament' and 'New Testament' are merely labels added to help us order the contents. Like history, poetry, prophecy, and so on.

Therefore, your Bible's covers encase a collection of writings produced over some 1,500 years by dozens of different authors. In gathering and ordering them, certain labels have been assigned for the purpose of communication. That includes the terms 'Bible', 'Old and New Testaments', and most of the book titles. Even the table of contents was added. All of this packaging is helpful because who would want to carry around all of those scrolls?

But the very packaging and labelling that is so essential to us will smother the contents if we let them. We must allow each writing to sound forth in its own voice, peeling back the packaging whenever we see it getting in the way. People who think the Bible isn't readable have just not pulled all the wrapping off. It's like trying to eat the sandwich while it's still in the plastic wrap.

Those who enjoy bananas know you don't have to eat the whole bunch and you don't have to eat the skin. You decide how hungry you are. You pick either a big one, or little one,

Figure 2.1

How the Bible Writers Refer to the Bible

The law of Moses
The law of the Lord
The law
The book of the law
Moses and the Prophets
The Prophets and Moses
The Prophets
Moses
The Law and the Prophets
The Scriptures of the Prophets
the holy Scriptures
the Scripture(s)
the sacred writings
The Law of Moses and the Prophets and the Psalms
It is written
the word of God
the word of the Lord

Note: In these cases, wherever the word 'law' is seen, the Jewish reference would be 'torah'.

or something in between. You pull the skin back. And you eat. And you watch out for those strands of the skin that sometimes stick to the banana. They have to be picked off.

None of this is too hard for us. It's no more difficult to read past labels and numbers than it is to read past those lines on the globe. And as you do this, the variety and vitality of the writings spring forth. You no longer see denominational bias or the publisher's style of packaging; it's living literature. You don't see dark caverns of print, but light and life. You'll still use the labels, but you'll use them in a way that doesn't let them mislead you. Individual writers will sound forth their common themes. Themes that touched the world when they were written, for centuries afterwards, and still today.

But even when we succeed in freeing the Bible from its wrapping, there are certain places in our reading where we can get bogged down. I'd like to show you how to avoid the bogs. Or if you get stuck, how to get out. Who knows? If Jesus could walk on water, maybe you and I can walk across bogs! Let me show you some of the common ones.

3

Modern Readers and an Ancient Bible

Now that we've peeled back the Bible's wrapping, we're ready for the enjoyable part. But as we take a bite, we sometimes find the flavour of what we're tasting, and even the texture of what we're chewing, a little different from what we're used to. Unless, that is, we're used to reading things written thousands of years ago. (That's another reason for all the wrapping: preserving the texture and flavour of what was written so long ago.)

Ancient writers wrote differently from modern writers. Ancient writers used different words and different phrasings. Their choice of subjects, focus, and even tone vary considerably from their modern counterparts. Bible translators go to some lengths to make these ancient writings look 'normal' to us. But there remains a style to ancient writing which distinguishes it from writing produced today. It's a simple style – so simple that we sometimes trip over it.

It doesn't take long to acquire a taste for the Bible's style. In many ways it's an easier adjustment than we have to make for some modern writers. The more you read the Bible, the more you get a feel for it. But until you get that exposure, let me point out approaches that will take some of the strangeness out of the reading.

Bridging the Distance of Time

Apart from specifics like names and dates, the Bible still has an ancient style which requires an adjustment on the part of modern readers. Almost two thousand years have elapsed since the last writing included in the Bible was completed. Do literary styles and the cultures that give rise to them change over time? I've struggled over Shakespeare's syntax, and he's only four centuries removed from me. I've even had a hard time with the dialect in Mark Twain's books, and he's only one century removed from me. Only the timelessness of the Bible's truths and the simplicity of its style can account for its still having a readership after all these years.

The Bible may have been written *for* posterity, but it was not written *to* posterity. It wasn't sealed in a time capsule with instructions to be opened in the year AD 2000. It was written to people of that day and age. For example, when we read the letters of the New Testament, we're reading correspondence between two parties. They make reference to situations, ideas, and customs that are unknown to us today. As long as we don't *expect* to understand every single allusion, we can read profitably. But if we expect every single line to make sense, as if it were a letter written directly to us, we'll be continually frustrated.

If you've ever looked at any old family correspondence, you know that not everything the writer makes reference to can be completely understood. Details become obscured by time. If correspondence acquires some vagueness in spots after only a generation or two, why should we expect every word of the Bible to make complete sense to us?

When you buy a mystery or romance novel at the airport or railway station, you can count on the book being written to you. It will use a vocabulary common to most people. If it makes reference to anything unfamiliar – customs, geography, or incidents – it will explain those references in the text. Now imagine that some of those books were preserved for some two thousand years into the future. Do you think people in AD 4000 will understand all the references you did? Of course not. They will be able to gain from the general storyline and much that accompanies it, for the passions and actions of humans endure through every age. As the Bible itself says, 'There is nothing new under the sun'. But much that is common knowledge now will be very ancient and possibly obscure by then.

The only way the Bible could have survived all these years is if it dealt with the unchanging issues of human existence: life, death, joy, sorrow, achievement, failure, and so on. Yet these issues are couched in the language of ancient times. Simply remembering this will keep your reading experience moving. Have you ever driven a car on an old cobbled road? As long as you slow down and expect some bumps, you find the road is quite satisfactory and will get you where you're going. But if you're used to a smooth tarmac motorway and don't slow down, the cobbled road will jar you.

The Bible as a whole is old, and its various parts are old to varying degrees. With well over a thousand years between the time of the first writing and the time of the last, there is plenty of opportunity for literary styles to change within the Bible's covers. Consider this: at least half as much time elapsed between the Bible's first book and its last, as has elapsed between its last book and now. That means you can expect the writing style to vary not just between modern books and the Bible, but between the Bible books themselves.

The best way to cope with the Bible's oldness and internal variations in style is to read . . . more . . . slowly . . . than . . . you . . . usually . . . do. Remember the cobbled road. By reading more slowly, you will be able to sense the rhythm in the writer's syntax. This will allow you to follow the thoughts and absorb more meaning. Though you won't complete as many pages in an hour of reading, you may find yourself coming away with far more knowledge and understanding per page than you are used to. The reason for this is that the Bible is very dense with ideas. When you read at a rapid clip, you simply can't process all you're reading.

While you're slowing down, don't slow down too much. You won't be able to enjoy that either. How much, then, do you slow down? You'll know as you're reading. The road itself lets you know how fast you can go. As you follow the flow of words on the paper, remembering to look past the wrapping, you'll sense the rhythm of the particular writing. This rhythm may even change within a particular book. Ancient writers may not have known the devices of the modern publishing industry, but they knew how to make the words carry the reader along.

Once you recognise that life is hard, it gets a little easier to manage. It's only when you think it's supposed to be easy that you find it unmanageably hard. Likewise, once you recognise that these ancient texts must be read slowly, then you can begin to read them faster. It's only when you think that they can be wolfed down in a hurry that you find them impossible to digest.

Designed for the Ear More Than the Eye

In antiquity, people read aloud even when reading to themselves. The silent reading we engage in today was largely unknown back then. This is but one facet of how much ancient literature, particularly that found in the Bible, was oriented for the ear more than the eye.

Consider that these writings were produced long before the age of the printing press and commercial publishing. Writing materials were much harder to come by, and photocopiers were in the far distant and unimaginable future. The way for writing to a mass audience was for it *to be read aloud*.

Today we think nothing of going to a nearby bookshop and buying a Bible if we choose. People in antiquity, even if they knew of the Bible, did not have this sort of access to it. It was far more likely that they would hear the words read at a religious festival. Therefore, if a survey had been taken in antiquity of everyone who was familiar with the Bible, the largest percentage of them would be familiar with it by ear, not by sight.

Those who wrote the Bible, therefore, did so knowing that their words would be read aloud. This affected the way they wrote. Written speech and spoken speech are in some ways two different languages. What works for one doesn't work for the other. Repetitions of a theme, for instance, can help a listener stay focused on the subject. But in silent reading, they can be annoying. That's why transcriptions of great speeches don't always carry the same impact as the original speech. And that's why reading the Bible these days doesn't always flow smoothly for us – it was written to be spoken aloud.

The genealogies which so often throw our reading out of gear were probably part of the author's way of keeping readers (that is, listeners) awake. The abrupt change of style and pace kept the text from monotony. And in books that tell about the kings, each new king was introduced and later dispensed with in a recurring refrain such as 'and King So-and-So died and slept with his fathers in the city of David'.

Such clues make it obvious that Bible writers knew how to avoid droning. If you've ever read aloud to a group, you know that the attention span of your hearers determines where you stop, more than any chapter divisions. By contrast, an individual silent reader uses the chapter divisions to pace the reading. He or she can see that there's just a page or two more and push him – or herself if necessary. Or see that the next chapter is very long so there's no sense starting it just now. Such visual clues are of no help to a listener. The writer might therefore use different cues, such as a well-placed genealogy or recurring refrain.

Not only was most of the Bible written with the intention of its being read aloud, much of it was verbal material before it was reduced to writing. Thus, the apostles' letters were written so that they could be read aloud to the groups to which they were addressed, and the stories in the books of Moses had been passed on orally from generation to generation before they were written down. Constantly bear in mind the auditory nature of the Bible. And if you ever get stuck at a particular passage, try reading it aloud and see if that doesn't help you over the hump.

Culture Shock Between Ages

The sheep, pastures, anointing oil, and such that are so prevalent in Bible times are not that common to us. Yet these aspects of culture and time don't usually shock our understanding. We frequently reach for novels to read which take us into realms with which we don't have daily contact. But there are some things that shock our sensibilities to such a degree that we must figure out how to deal with them.

The Bible speaks about miracles without making apology or even stirring up its tone. In other words, it doesn't anticipate scepticism. It considers the whole creation rather miraculous. Therefore, it shows the same awe for a sunrise as it does for a day when the sun stands still. It drops its jaw in wonder at *any* human birth – not just the ones where a father or both parents were absent. It regards our entire existence as a miracle, and what we today call miracles as momentary departures from the normal course of that miracle. Modern writing generally doesn't take this approach. Any mention of the miraculous usually expects challenge and therefore offers some proof or explanation. So this is an adjustment you have to make as a reader.

That is part of the reason I am attempting to present the Bible to you at its face value. That is, I am not second-guessing every passage, telling you to take *this* seriously but not *that*. Bible scholars can often get defensive about the Bible. They realise certain things are hard for the modern mind to accept and try to compensate by telling the reader what can be regarded as trustworthy and what can't. As a result, the poor reader is bombarded by archaelogical facts and scholarly theories, and thus loses track of which lines are supposed to be reliable and which aren't. I think it's far better to take the text at face value and let it speak for itself. When a book lacks integrity, most readers are discriminating enough to notice it. If the Bible lacked integrity, it would have passed from the scene long ago.

Another big area of culture shock has come to be the issue of gender equality. Writers go to great pains in our day to keep any hint of gender bias from reaching the pages. Those writers who fail, and particularly those who don't even try, are scoffed at and generally not read at all. For this reason, some new Bible translations attempt, among other things, to eliminate all the masculine references to God. As you become familiar with the Bible, however, you will see that it supports gender equality without having to resort to such extreme measures.

First, the male-female relationships in the Bible do – compared to our present-day standards – seem to put women in a subordinate position to men. But when you compare the Bible to the standards of the day in which it was written, you will see that it was always lifting women up. It was continually giving them a better place in life than that culture was allowing them.

Second, eradicating the masculine references to God strips the Bible of some of its most beautiful and compelling imagery concerning God and humanity. Our relationship with God is to be one of mutual enthralment. We love Him and He loves us: a marriage with enormous possibilities for happiness and fruitfulness.

But more than miracles and female equality, the issue of polytheism is the one that distinguishes our age from that of the Bible. It was only subsequent to the time of the Bible that monotheism became the dominant Western worldview. It's so common now, that many of us don't give it a second thought. Only when we read ancient literature do we realise that things weren't always this way. It is amazing that we borrow from the ancient Greeks and Romans so many ideas without even taking seriously their ideas about multiple gods. We call that mythology.

Today an atheist says that he or she doesn't believe in God – not gods. Antiquity knew no such atheists. Everyone and every nation had a god of their own, and usually more than one. Times have changed, but the Bible takes us back to the way things were.

But the redeeming and fascinating thing about the Bible is that it was written from a monotheistic view even in those polytheistic times. Therefore, it doesn't seem so strange to us after all. But it helps to remember that the monotheism being proclaimed by the Bible was considered very strange by the surrounding cultures. This radical difference of worldviews explains much of the conflict and tension in the Bible stories and in the outworking of Israelite history.

Unfamiliar Names for Persons, Places, and Things

The Bible is full of names. Many of these names are ones with which we're unfamiliar. And this unfamiliarity sometimes is a stumbling block to our reading. But the stumbling can be avoided by remembering a few things.

The Bible is as much about people as it is about God. People are people; the strangeness of some of their names has only to do with their different culture, language, and the time in which they lived. That doesn't mean our reading has to be hindered – it can be enhanced by such specifics. A name like 'Hamlet' can become all the more charming and memorable precisely because so few of the children on today's playgrounds respond when you call it out. And though the name 'Habbakuk' may seem a little strange to some of us, it certainly meant something special to his mum and dad. Besides, we are always no more than a generation away from seeing an obscure name become a common one. Let someone with an unusual name become famous, and a generation of babies will make the name usual.

Besides, many of the names found in the Bible are familiar to us: Mary, Joseph, Elizabeth, John, and so on. We ourselves choose many of these names for our children. On the other hand, not too many parents name their children Job, or Methuselah, or Obadiah, and certainly not Habakkuk. At least not in our generation. Of course, these things have a way of changing. Children's names that were commonly given in the time you and I were growing up are often replaced by others in the next generation (the 'Barbara's of one generation are replaced by the 'Jennifer's of the next). And so who knows what children will be commonly called in the generation to come?

Surnames, as we know them, aren't found in the Bible. But we can find the seeds of them. For example, you'll find the name 'Solomon the son of David' in the books about Israel's kings. It wouldn't be strange in our day to meet someone named 'Solomon Davidson'. Likewise, the Bible may call someone 'Joseph the son of Jacob' while we today call him 'Joe Jacobson'. It's a short hop from 'son of John' to 'Johnson' – one of the most common surnames in the English-speaking world.

Surnames come not just from the parents, but from the occupation of a person or family. Therefore, people we know today as 'Dave Shepherd' or 'Joe Carpenter' might have been called 'David the shepherd' or 'Joseph the carpenter'. Surnames also come from one's city or village. Recognising how surnames have arisen make us realise that ancient names aren't that different from our own.

Even if you're used to keeping up with national destinies on the evening news, you're still not used to hearing biblical names like the Midianites, Amalekites, Philistines, and so on. Only remnants remain of these ancient cultures, and sometimes not even that much. But just as Americans are people from America, and English are people from England, so Midianites were people from Midian and Amalekites were people from Amalek. Modern-day remnants of ancient cultures are usually called by slightly different names to keep the chronology straight. Therefore, inhabitants of ancient Israel were called Israelites, while inhabitants of modern Israel are called Israelis.

Place names in the Bible often came from the person or people who settled the area. Thus the land of Israel derived its name from the man whose descendants inhabited it: Israel. Earlier, the land had been called by the name of the man whose descendants inhabited it: Canaan. Though many of these names are unfamiliar to us, certainly this way of naming places is not.

You can become overwhelmed by the sheer number of names in the Bible. It catalogues thousands of people and places. But just as certain stars shine brighter than others in the sky, so certain of these names shine brighter in the text. As you see them repeated again and again, they make an impression that sticks. The city of Jerusalem, most notably, figures as the most prominent place throughout the centuries that the Bible records history. Pay attention to the place names that are repeated and don't spend much time pondering places that aren't. The same goes for people mentioned in the Bible.

One more thing about people and places. The Bible writings were written primarily for the people of Israel. These documents were part and parcel of their lives and documented all their ancestors and their homeland. You can't expect yourself to keep up with all the details as well as the original readers could. But while we can't identify all the trees that they could, we can see the forest better from this distance in time. Being able to recognise larger themes and trends in the Bible writings is the advantage of being a modern reader.

So much for the unfamiliar names of people and places that fill the Bible. Now a brief word about unfamiliar names of things. Ever called something a 'whatchamacallit' or a 'thingamajig'? When the ancient Israelites first encountered God's miraculous provision of food in the desert, they used such a term. When the morning dew evaporated, on the surface of the ground was 'a fine flake-like thing, fine as frost'. They called it 'manna' which literally means 'What is it?' In other words, they called this stuff on the ground 'whatchamacallit'. You just can't help relating to people like that – they're too much like us!

A Word about Pronouncing These Strange Names

The Bible's unfamiliar words may cause us additional problems when we try to pronounce them. The fear of embarrassing yourself by mispronouncing a Bible word may inhibit your bringing up the Bible as a topic for discussion. Here are a few facts which should help you put that fear to rest.

First, I have mispronounced many Bible names and given my hearers many a laugh. Nevertheless, I live; none of these experiences have proved fatal. Second, pronunciation is a subjective judgment anyway since all these words were penned long, long before any of us was born. How can anyone say with absolute certainty how the ancients pronounced all these words? Third, we speak English – a language foreign to the Bible. Linguists know that modern Hebrew and modern Greek often differ in pronunciation from their ancient counterparts – how much more would English pronunciation differ?

Most of the words in the Bible will be familiar to you: Judges, Matthew, Timothy. You don't pronounce them differently just because they're in the Bible. As for the unfamiliar words, sound them out the same way you would an unfamiliar word found anywhere else.

One special note: 'ch', which is commonly found, is almost always pronounced with a 'k' sound. Therefore the first syllable of Zechariah is pronounced 'zeck', and the last syllable of Malachi is pronounced 'kye'. One exception is cherub, the name for a certain kind of angel, in which the 'ch' is sounded like the 'ch' of chair. And speaking of cherub, cherubim is the plural. The 'im' ending acts as an 's' or 'es' ending.

If you're uncomfortable going it alone on pronunciation, you can always refer to a dictionary where all the Bible book titles and many of the individual names are included. But even that's no guarantee. I'm from South Carolina and we often find dictionaries giving the 'incorrect' pronunciation of certain words! Anyway, these ancient languages are now 'dead'. There's no one around to verify the official pronunciation. Why should we refrain from discussing the Bible just because someone might make fun of the way we render a given name? Such mockery is petty.

Dates

The Bible way of dating things is not so different from ours . . . but it seems so. For example, we are used to seeing numbers like 1984 or 2001. Not only does the Bible not give numbers like these, it does not even use the terms 'BC' or 'AD'. Instead, we encounter phrases like:

> In the four hundred and eightieth year after the Israelites had come out of Egypt, in the fourth year of Solomon's reign over Israel, in the month of Ziv, the second month, he . . .

> 1 Kings 6:1

Israel gave the months different names from the ones we use today – but this was true of all ancient cultures. And the unfamiliarity of 'Ziv' is overcome by the presence of the familiar word 'second'. The mentioning of Solomon and the exodus from Egypt relate the story at hand to other points of interest in the Bible.

This method of dating connects Bible events to each other, but not to events in our time. But this is okay, as long as we're not expecting our normal method of dating to appear. Yet our method of dating is essentially the same as theirs. For when we say 'AD 2000' we are saying 'In the two-thousandth year of Christ' – 'Anno Domini' being Latin for 'in the year of the Lord'. And important documents are sometimes further dated with a reference to the number of years elapsed since the founding of the nation. For example, in the United States, the Constitution is dated 'in the year of our Lord one thousand seven hundred and eighty seven and of the Independence of the United States of America the twelfth'. Therefore, a date like 1994 is merely shorthand. We count time from important events just like they did in Bible times.

Lively Passages

Let's consider that, to the unfamiliar reader, every passage of the Bible can be described as either lively or tedious. I'll mention some of the more tedious passages and strategies for negotiating them. But first let me say something about the lively passages. You won't need me to say much, because their very liveliness means they read easily without explanation.

The liveliest passages in the Bible are the stories. They are about people and they are full of action – two ingredients for the easiest reading. But even here a moderated reading speed will help you. The reason is that the stories are remarkably concise – you could even say terse and pithy – compared to modern standards.

For example, consider this passage from the story of Joseph and his brothers:

Now his brothers had gone to graze their father's flocks near Shechem, and Israel said to Joseph, 'As you know, your brothers are grazing the flocks near Shechem. Come, I am going to send you to them.'

'Very well,' he replied.

So he said to him, 'Go and see if all is well with your brothers and with the flocks, and bring word back to me.' Then he sent him off from the valley of Hebron.

When Joseph arrived at Shechem, a man found him wandering around in the fields, and asked him, 'What are you looking for?'

He replied, 'I'm looking for my brothers. Can you tell me where they are grazing their flocks?'

Genesis 37:12–16

So-and-so did, so-and-so said – nothing much else. This manner of storytelling is typical of the Bible's narrative passages.

We are used to reading novels and even historical accounts that go into much more detail about what so-and-so thought and felt. Also, we are used to seeing a much more detailed description of the scenery. In comparison to most novels, the Bible is a barebones, 'just the facts' sort of approach. There are times when motives, feelings, and inward thoughts are revealed. But such revelations are infrequent and well timed. The Bible uses them like salt on a meal: none at all makes the meal too bland, but it's easy to add too much and spoil the flavour of the different foods.

The modern novelist or historian does much of our thinking for us, and a good one has us reaching for the next page continually. But those who wrote the Bible wrote in such a way that a reader must slow down and linger. The reader must reflect, interact, ponder. Bible stories usually existed in oral form before they were written down. This helps account for their compactness. You will get the most from them by reading them as if you were listening to them told around a table or a campfire. The story keeps your imagination churning and makes for a dramatic experience.

Other lively passages include much of the poetry, although it isn't always easy to understand. There are also the straight-forward teaching passages, of which there are many in the Bible. Passages such as: 'Love your neighbour as yourself'. However difficult such passages may be to practise, they aren't difficult to read. In fact, what makes Jesus's teaching so challenging – lines such as, 'If someone strikes you on the right cheek, turn to him the other also' – is that the words are so plain.

Tedious Passages

The Bible is more than a collection of stories and teachings. It's also a collection of important information that, for all its value, can be difficult to read. In modern books, such information is usually tucked away in an appendix. But in the Bible, such passages may show up anywhere in the text. For instance, the story of Joseph quoted above comes just after a chapter-long genealogical list. For this reason, let me list and describe some of the more common types of tedious passages and how to deal with them when they pop up.

Genealogies. Normally, a genealogy is intensely interesting – if it's your own. Otherwise, it's a yawn. So-and-so begat so-and-so. Who cares? For this reason, the first strategy for dealing with genealogies in the Bible is to pass over them. Otherwise, they can quickly bog down your reading.

Here's a genealogy taken from one of the gospels:

A record of the genealogy of Jesus Christ, the son of David, the son of Abraham:

Abraham was the father of Isaac,
Isaac was the father of Jacob,
Jacob the father of Judah and his brothers,
Judah the father of Perez and Zerah, whose mother was Tamar,
Perez the father of . . .

Matthew 1:1–3

And on it goes for another umpteen lines. We are used to seeing writing like this in the county records, or even in the phone book. But we are not used to curling up in a soft chair with it. As you begin to read the Bible, therefore, it's wise to fast-forward the tape when you come to lines like these. They never go on indefinitely, and when they end, the action always picks back up.

You might feel a little guilty as you do this sort of skipping and skimming. Many of us were taught to eat everything on our plates – including the vegetables. And your guilt may be accompanied by an anxiety over the possibility that you may be passing over some point essential to the story preceding or following it. The guilt and anxiety are understandable but not necessary. Like a phone book, nothing will be more important to you than a genealogy, once you have a need for the information it contains. But until you have that need, nothing will be more boring to read.

When will the need arise, you ask, for the information in a genealogy? Once you've gained enough interest in the stories that precede and follow it. Take, for example, the genealogy of Jesus that we read. If you read some of the stories about Him in Matthew's Gospel, you may want to come back and read this genealogy. It provides background to explain such questions as why He was sometimes called 'Son of David'. And why Jesus's relationship to Abraham is important. In other words, the names don't mean much to you as you simply read them in a list. But once you've read the story and are able to 'put a face to a name', so to speak, the place in the genealogy begins to provide meaning.

Why are the genealogies there in the first place? As we've seen, the Bible was ancient Israel's official book. This would account for the presence of some of these lists. Moreover, ancient Israel itself, remember, was a result of God's promise to a man named Abraham *and his descendants*. Being able to trace one's heritage to Abraham was, therefore, of enormous importance. Those who became priests to serve in the tabernacle and temple were required to prove descent from a particular descendant of Abraham. For these reasons alone, it was in the national interest to keep genealogical records. Thus, we find them strewn throughout the Bible.

The more you read the Bible, the more you will find the genealogical lists of interest. For the more names become familiar to you, the more their presence in the list stands out to you. That leads you to connect who came before them to who came after them. Thus, the Bible stories cease to be a disconnected jumble as you develop a historical perspective in which to place each of them. In other words, no one will have to tell you to read them; you'll want to. Therefore, my word to you until then: Don't bother reading them.

Census Lists and Numbers. A close cousin to the genealogy is the census. As ancient Israel's population grew, the Bible kept track of it. Individuals grew into families, families into tribes, and the tribes into a nation. At each stage, you find the Bible listing names and numbers associated with those names. Here's an example:

> The list of the men of Israel:

the descendants of Parosh	2,172
of Shephatiah	372
of Arah	652
of Pahath-Moab (through the line of Jeshua and Joab)	2,818
of Elam	1,254
of Zattu,	845 . . .

Nehemiah 7:7–13

And on it goes for at least another fifty lines. This census shows up smack in the middle of Nehemiah's storytelling. If you're not prepared to fast-forward through it, as I've recommended with genealogies, you could get bogged down. Then you'd never get to Nehemiah's other lively stories just beyond it.

As with genealogies, the time may come when you are interested in these details. But even then, you will probably read such passages as you would a phone book (selectively) – not as you would a novel (sequentially).

These census lists are also of value apart from the mass of details they provide about individuals, families, and tribes. When compared to each other in general terms, they give a feel for the growth or decline of the nation of Israel. The numbers tell a story. Increasing numbers testify to the growing prosperity of the descendants of Israel. Decreasing numbers bear witness to the toll of famine and war. The Bible's narrative portions are thus reinforced and dramatised further by these statistics. Only when viewed by themselves are they dry numbers.

Dimensions for Building. When God told Noah to build the ark, the instructions were recorded in the book of Genesis. In the first place, we might prefer to see such instructions in the form of a blueprint. It takes a lot of words to convey the same image that a clearly drawn diagram would provide. But there are no drawings in the Bible, except those added by modern scholars. Ancient writers left us only words – lots of them.

But then, since God has promised in the Bible to never send another flood like the one Noah faced, we don't need a diagram or description. Of course there are other reasons we might be glad to have the dimensions of that ark. But most of us readers will find such information mildly interesting at best. Fast-forward time again.

Not only does the Bible contain dimensions for building the ark, it contains dimensions for other major building projects that God commissioned. Moses' writings contain a great deal of such information because he was told to build a tabernacle complete with furnishings. Centuries later, Solomon built a permanent temple in Jerusalem to replace that portable structure. We have dimensions for that building, too. Be forewarned: there are such passages in the Bible. When you encounter them, you know what to do.

Boundary Descriptions. Just as there could have been a blueprint of Noah's ark, so there could have been a map of Bible lands. The Bible writers left us neither. When they wanted to delineate the borders of Israel, they used words describing well-known (to them) landmarks such as rivers, mountains, and deserts. This applied not only to the external borders of the nation, but the internal borders of its various provinces. The maps that are in our Bibles have been prepared by modern scholars based on these descriptions. Obviously, such 'word maps' made for lengthy descriptions. We modern readers can only find them tedious, until we are more familiar with the landmarks referred to.

Detailed Ritual and Legal Code. Israel was a unique nation, called to render service to the other nations of the world. As such, this nation had a priesthood which kept the furnishings of the tabernacle, and later the temple, and performed rituals of sacrifice and purification. All these detailed instructions are found in the Scriptures, but they won't be of immediate interest to most readers.

Ancient Israelites who were not priests still had a number of detailed regulations which were required of them as members of this unique nation. There were particular feasts that had to be kept, particular foods that could and could not be eaten, particular sacrifices that were to be offered. The tabernacle, or temple, around which all this activity revolved no longer exists. Further, we are ages removed from the time when these practices were standard. It only stands to reason that our interest in them will not be as great. We can find and extract principles of moral living from these rituals and regulations, but that usually comes after we have become more familiar with the stories and general teachings of the Bible.

Repetitive passages. We modern readers find repetition in a book annoying. But remember that the Bible is an anthology, and some repetition between authors is not only unavoidable, it's actually authenticating . . . and, therefore, desirable. For example, two witnesses testifying to crucial facts in a trial strengthen the court's reliance on those facts.

Also, repeated passages sometimes give additional details which were absent in the original passage. Sometimes it's hard to reconcile all the myriad details in these accounts.

But this fact, too, attests to their reliability. For when two witnesses testify identically in every single respect, the smell of a fabrication is in the air. Nevertheless, once you notice you're reading a repetitious passage, you'll probably want to skim through until you reach some fresh material. The benefits of such duplicate or parallel passages probably won't be important to you in your Bible-reading excursions.

Finding a Place to Get Started

The first chapter of this book was about the Bible's structure. Understanding its structure makes the Bible more accessible. The second chapter was about wrapping. Distinguishing the wrapping from the writing makes the Bible more readable. This chapter was about the texture of the writing – while much of it is meaty, there is some gristle that can spoil it. If we can avoid passages that seem like detours, our Bible reading will be more enjoyable. To find the Bible accessible, readable, and enjoyable is, thus, possible for all of us.

There are lively books and tedious books. But more often there are lively books with some tedious passages and tedious books with some lively passages. You are now better prepared to negotiate your way, no matter where you are reading in the Bible.

Still, you must start your reading somewhere. If not at the beginning, then where? The best way to decide is to take a closer look at each book in the Bible. That's what the next part of this book will give you. Each of the next seven chapters tackles a section of the Bible's writings. In reading those chapters, you will receive a clearer impression of the books that make up the Bible, the order in which they're found, and the nature of each individual book. You'll get some good ideas about where you want to begin, and continue, your Bible reading.

In the beginning of this book I gave you a quick tour of the Bible's library. Now let's go back through and browse a little more thoroughly. If you're anxious to begin reading the Bible itself and already know where you want to start, you can jump to the appropriate chapter in Part Two, orient yourself, and begin reading your desired Bible book. You can catch up with the browsing later. And you can jump to Part Three any time you want. If you have time, let's go through Parts Two and Three, step by step.

Part Two

The Parts of the Bible

4

The Books of Moses

The first section of Bible books we want to look at in more detail is the Law of Moses. These five books are not only the first we find upon peeling back the Bible's cover, they are the original Bible – the cornerstone of all the books contributed by later generations. But just because these books are the Bible's first – physically and logically – does not mean they are where everyone's Bible reading should begin. For while their pages include some of the most delightful passages in all the world's literature, they also include some of the most difficult.

Size and Scope

If the whole Bible is as long as ten books, this section is equal to two. So we're still dealing with something sizable. Let's consider the Bible as the world, with each of its sections like one of the continents. The books of Moses can be likened to Africa – vast and varied. Within its huge expanse we find dry deserts but also lush forests; scorching winds but also teeming rivers. And while the terrain is sometimes forbidding, there are rich mineral deposits waiting below. Its vastness is matched only by its variety. While Africa is no place for the timid, it is a paradise for those who embrace it.

The point is that, even though we are breaking down the Bible and dealing with it a section at a time, each section still can be intimidating by itself – especially the five books attributed to Moses. You can visit a small part of Africa or you can cover every foot of it – the choice is yours. But if you don't properly appreciate its size and scope, you're liable to get lost in it.

The Names of the Books

The names of the five books – *Genesis, Exodus, Leviticus, Numbers,* and *Deuteronomy* – come from the subject matter found in each. '*Genesis*' comes from a word meaning 'to be born'. From that same word we also get words like 'genetic', 'congenital', and 'genealogy'. The book of *Genesis* marks the beginning of the Bible and describes the beginning of creation. Within its pages are also found the beginnings, or seeds, of many ideas which grow in later Bible books.

'*Exodus*' comes from two words: the first meaning 'our of' and the second meaning 'way'. Together they communicate 'the way out of'. This speaks of the Israelites finding their way out of slavery in Egypt, and this story is told in the book of *Exodus*.

'*Leviticus*' derives its name from 'Levite'. The Levites were that tribe of Israelites who were chosen for special service to the whole nation. To this tribe were entrusted all the details of the national religion, including animal sacrifice. Since many of those details were recorded in this book, it came to be called *Leviticus*.

The book of *Numbers* begins and ends with a census of the Israelites. For this reason it is called '*Numbers*', although there is much more to the book than that. This is a good place to remember that Bible book titles are strictly for reference. Unlike modern book titles, they arose long after the books did and were not intended to encapsulate the books or entice interest.

Deuteronomy, the last of the five books usually credited to Moses, repeats much that is in the books before it. For example, the Ten Commandments, first given in Exodus, are repeated here. The word '*Deuteronomy*' comes from two words: one meaning 'second' and the other meaning 'law'. In other words, it was a second giving of the law, a repetition. Again, though the title has to do with the content, it hardly does it justice, for there is much more to the book than this.

How the Five Books Fit Together

Stretch out the fingers of your right hand with your palm facing away from you. This will tell you something about how the five books of Moses relate to each other. First, the five parts belong to one whole. Second, though the five parts bear some resemblance to each other, they are hardly identical. Last, the four on the right have more in common with each other than with the one on the left.

Genesis is the book on the left. It is the thumb. The books from *Exodus* to *Deuteronomy* all describe events contemporary with Moses. *Genesis*, however, reaches back into history to describe origins – the origin of the universe, the origin of the Israelites, and so on. Moses could speak as an eyewitness and participant of many of the events described in books two to five. The books from *Exodus* to *Deuteronomy* cover the events of his lifetime (albeit a lengthy one – Moses lived to be 120). Genesis, on the other hand, summarises the events of thousands of years. Therefore, we are told a great deal about the time of Moses compared to the highlights we're given of all the generations that preceded him. But while the thumb may be the most different of the five fingers, it is the one that most helps them operate together as a hand. Likewise, the books of Moses would be seriously handicapped without Genesis.

The Law of Moses was spawned by a great event: the birth of the nation of Israel. These documents, then, can be considered a sort of national birth certificate. Each nation has its own unique origin. Take, for example, the birth of the United States. Though its history is unlike Israel's in many ways, the Declaration of Independence and Constitution function in a similar way to the writings of Moses. Both Israel's documents and America's were produced in the context of a nation being founded. Both sought to provide legitimacy for the nation. Both were shaped by the thinking of great leaders who risked much to secure freedom for the new country. And although the ideas in the Declaration of Independence and Constitution may have been around long before the documents themselves, it was the formation of a new nation which caused those documents to come into being and to be treasured by subsequent generations. So it was with the books of Moses.

Associating the books of Moses with the nation whose birth they directed and chronicled will help you keep the history straight as you view the individual books. Those who study the Declaration and Constitution learn to distinguish the related but distinct purposes of each document. Likewise, each of our fingers has a distinct but related purpose. So it is with *Genesis, Exodus, Leviticus, Numbers,* and *Deuteronomy.*

Genesis

If the Law of Moses is Africa, then *Genesis* is its largest region, being at least 20 per cent larger than any of the others. By now you see the problem clearly. The unsuspecting reader opens her Bible to page one. She finds the story of creation, which does not surprise her as a way for God's book to start. But it won't be too many chapters before she's worn down by genealogies, obscure names, and a disappearing story line. Having landed on the coast of Africa with the greatest hopes for adventure and discovery, she soon gives up, discouraged and unable to complete the journey.

But by now you also see the solution clearly. The way to look at *Genesis* is not merely to begin and look forwards, but to stand at *Exodus* and look back. Moses is writing for his fellow Israelite slaves. As they struggle with Egypt's oppression, Moses answers the question, 'How did we get in this mess?' *Genesis* is the answer to that question. It tells the story of the Israelites' ancestors – all the way back to the first human beings. Moses is not trying to give the history of the whole world, but of his people. Sometimes that involved events of worldwide significance like creation and the flood. But it might just as well involve seemingly insignificant events like the sale of some stew and a young boy's dreams.

Genesis is background and prologue to all that happens from

Exodus to *Deuteronomy*. Details that it gives are important to that purpose; details that it omits are unimportant to that purpose. If it were to be written in our day, it would doubtless be constructed along different lines, and it wouldn't seem so strange to us. But that's the 'problem' with ancient literature: it's so . . . ancient. As you become more familiar with *Genesis*, however, you will come to appreciate its contours.

I will, from this point on, use chapter numbers like signposts on a motorway. It's the same idea as latitude and longitude lines, but at this stage of the journey we need arbitrary markers we can see by the road. But don't worry that I'll call out every one – with fifty chapters in *Genesis* and 1,189 in the Bible, you'll only want a few well chosen ones mentioned.

Genesis 1 and 2 tell the story of creation. In December of 1968, astronauts first broke the gravitational pull of earth and saw the far side of the moon. Coming around the moon they saw and took pictures of 'the first earthrise', the earth appearing over the lunar horizon. With millions of people attending by television and radio, the astronauts chose to mark the occasion by reading from these chapters: 'In the beginning God created . . .' So much for the supposed incompatibility of the Bible and science.

Genesis 3 tells of the disobedience of Adam and Eve in the garden of Eden, and chapter 4 tells of Cain murdering his brother Abel. Of all the things that give us trouble in relating to Adam and Eve as real people, failing to obey an instruction is not one of them. And while we can't all relate to the murder of Abel, we are all too familiar with the jealousy, anger, and hatred which inspired it. *Genesis* is about people. And though these ancient people may eat differently and speak differently and work differently from us, they still eat and speak and work. People are our common bond with *Genesis* . . . and with the rest of the Bible.

Genesis 5 gives a chapter-long genealogy. But, as you've learned, that requires no more of a reader than fast-forwarding the tape to the next action scene. Unless, that is, there is something in the genealogy that interests you. This one leads from Adam down to Noah.

Genesis 6 to 9 gives the account of Noah and the flood. Chapter 10 gives another genealogy, this one listing the descendants of Noah's three sons. The first part of chapter 11 tells about the Tower of Babel; the other part gives a genealogy leading from Noah down to Abraham.

All of *Genesis* that we have seen so far is a prologue to the book's central figure: Abraham. His story is the heart of the book, told from chapter 12 to 25. All that comes before is a context for understanding him. And all that comes after is understood in terms of the relationship God formed with him. Abraham had a son named Isaac, and Isaac had a son named Jacob. In a broader sense, the book of *Genesis* is about Abraham, Isaac, and Jacob. Or we might say the God of Abraham, Isaac, and Jacob. The Israelites who lived in the time of *Exodus*, waiting for deliverance from slavery, considered these details about their ancestors of enormous importance and relevance. As you read the stories you begin to see how they are connected to each other. And the more you read, the more connections you'll see.

God chose to make certain promises to Abraham. Most striking of these promises was one about a son and many descendants. This was striking because Abraham was childless and seventy-five years old when God made him the promise, and a hundred years old before it was fulfilled. His wife Sarah was only ten years younger than he. Oh, and don't be thrown off by the names Abram and Sarai when you're reading. These were their names at the beginning of the story, but in Genesis 17 God changes their names to Abraham and Sarah as a sign of His work in their lives.

Genesis 18 and 19 tell of the infamous Sodom and Gomorrah. In Genesis 21 the long awaited son Isaac is born. Genesis 22 tells how Abraham faced the test of sacrificing Isaac. He passed the test and was spared the ordeal of losing the son for whom he'd waited so long.

The storyline of *Genesis* continues with Isaac and particularly with his twin sons: Esau and Jacob. Though Esau was the firstborn and, therefore, designated by the custom of those times to receive the greater inheritance, Jacob sold him a bowl of stew in exchange for that birthright. This seemingly obscure incident was to have enormous consequences for the Israelites who would later trace their ancestry back to Jacob and not Esau.

Jacob managed to have twelve sons – a significant instalment in God's promise to give Abraham many descendants. One of Jacob's sons had some dreams about his own place in the scheme of things. His name was Joseph, and he is the focus of attention from Genesis 37 to the end of the book. When he told the dreams to the rest of the family, it intensified an already existing sibling rivalry. For all his shrewdness, Jacob could not escape many struggles in life, and his children supplied some of the more trying ones.

Although at first angry enough to kill Joseph, his brothers finally agreed to sell him as a slave to some travelling merchants. He ended up in Egypt. Joseph overcame great difficulty and eventually became vice-regent of all Egypt. Years later, his father and brothers were reconciled with him, and all joined him to live in the honour, peace, and prosperity of Egypt. So ends the book that sets the stage for *Exodus*.

Exodus

Exodus opens several hundred years after the close of *Genesis*. Jacob and seventy-odd family members have grown into the hundreds of thousands. The promise of descendants to Abraham may have seemed slow going in the beginning, but it received a jump-start when Jacob had twelve sons. Such a population explosion in one generation has a compounding effect in subsequent generations.

The term 'Israelites' simply meant that these people were descendants of a man named Israel. Israel was the additional name God had given Jacob (much the same as He had changed Abram's name to Abraham). Therefore, whether you read 'sons of Jacob' or 'Israelites', the meaning is the same. They might just as easily have been called 'Abrahamites', but 'Israelites' was the name that stuck.

The central theme of the book of *Genesis* – that a man named

Abraham would have descendants – is shown to have dramatic fulfilment. So dramatic that Egypt is crawling with them. An Egypt that could be gracious to Joseph's family when they numbered fewer than a hundred found them intimidating in larger numbers. Over the centuries, these privileged servants of Pharaoh were reduced to despised slaves.

The first two chapters of *Exodus* tell of Moses' early life. By Exodus 3 and 4 he is living in the desert, exiled from the Egypt of his birth. He sees a burning bush which was not being consumed by the fire. Drawing near to the intriguing sight, he hears the voice of God commissioning him to return to Egypt and bring the Israelites out of slavery.

In Exodus 5 Moses delivers the news to the then reigning Pharaoh (Pharaoh was not a personal name but the title of the king of Egypt): 'This is what the LORD, the God of Israel, says: "Let my people go, so that they may hold a festival to me in the desert."' Pharoah did not take kindly to the idea of losing an important part of his economy – free labour. As a result, there was a prolonged period of misery in Egypt as God brought plague after plague, designed to induce Pharaoh to give up his hold on the descendants of Abraham. All this is told in Exodus 5 to 12. At the tenth calamity, the death of all Egypt's firstborn children, Pharaoh relented, and the Israelites packed up their belongings and headed out of town for a new life.

God's promises to Abraham involved more than descendants. Those promises also covered the very practical matter of a land for those descendants to live on. Thus the term, 'the promised land'. In those days that land was called Canaan, after its original settlers. It sat to the north-east of Egypt. Today we call that area Palestine or Israel. This was the Israelites' ultimate destination, although their short-term goal was the wilderness (desert) which was east of Egypt and south of Canaan. Your Bible probably has maps that will help you.

As the Israelites left Egypt for the wilderness, Pharaoh determined once again that he would not let them go. He chased them down, and this set up the crossing of the Red Sea, which is recorded in Exodus 13 to 15. While the waters parted for the fleeing Israelites, they were not nearly so hospitable to the pursuing Egyptians. Pharaoh and his army were drowned. The days of slavery were over, but trouble would now take on new forms.

Chapters 16 to 19 tell of Israel's initial experiences in the desert. It was no picnic. The people quarrelled with Moses, with God, and with each other. Even springs of water from a rock and bread from heaven (manna) failed to quieten all the complaining. Some of the Israelites even wished to go back to Egypt. But Moses had brought them too far to turn around now. Exodus 20 records the moment at Mount Sinai when God, in the midst of fire and smoke, gave ten commandments to Moses to be given to the people. It was the burning bush experience revisited and magnified, with a larger cast of characters. Moses may have doubted that he could bring the people out, but now, having come full circle, all doubts bowed before the facts.

Beginning with Exodus 21, we encounter various detailed laws for the nation. Reading these will demand a bigger adjustment than any you have made so far. *Genesis* and *Exodus* up to this point have consisted largely of stories. Good stories are easy to read, and the verdict of history is that the ones in *Genesis* and *Exodus* are as good as they come. But when, following the Ten Commandments, Moses begins to pronounce a detailed legal code for the new nation, the avid Bible story reader may feel as if the train has been derailed. And there are no signs to indicate how it happened or when the rails might be found again. This is where most Bible readers pack it in. (Few people enjoy reading tax regulations.) For to pass over a few lines or even a whole chapter of genealogy is one thing, but to search through chapter after chapter of regulations that don't immediately apply to you, and hope for a breath of fresh air, is quite another.

From chapter 21 to the end of *Exodus*, only chapter 24 and chapters 32 to 34 (the golden calf incident) offer significant action. The rest of the book is taken up with details about laws, national festivals, and so on. The largest portion is given to instructions about how to build the tabernacle – a portable temple for God. Given the complexity of instructions about how to assemble a bicycle, you can imagine how tedious these instructions must be. Consider also that Moses left no drawings – all the instructions were words. Imagine bicycle assembly instructions with no pictures!

You can avoid being suffocated by these passages if you learn to steer around them. For this reason, you may want to consider taking a pencil to your Bible and marking off these passages of 'quicksand'. The boundaries will change as you read more of the Bible, but if you don't note these sections now, you probably won't read more of the Bible. As has been said, don't consider these dense passages worthless – just parts of the 'newspaper' in which you are not yet interested.

Leviticus

While *Genesis* is chock-full of stories and *Exodus* is half-full of them, *Leviticus* is almost devoid of them. The kind of detailed regulations and instructions we found in the last half of *Exodus* are about all we see in *Leviticus*. Consider the opening lines:

> The LORD called to Moses and spoke to him from the Tent of Meeting. He said, "Speak to the Israelites and say to them: 'When any of you brings an offering to the LORD, either bring as your offering an animal from the herd or the flock.
>
> "'If the offering is a burnt offering from the herd, he is to offer a male without defect. He must present it at the entrance to the Tent of Meeting so that it will be acceptable to the LORD. He is to lay his hand on the head of the burnt offering, and it will be accepted on his behalf to make atonement for him.'"
>
> Leviticus 1:1–4

The text goes on like this, page after page, seven chapters' worth. For people wanting to sacrifice animals it makes perfect sense, but for people wanting to extract principles, it's tough going. From Leviticus 8 to 10 we read of the ordination of the priests of Israel. The priests were a subset of the Levites, just as the Levites were a subset of the Israelites. As the Levites were to keep the tabernacle and all its services for the rest of the nation, so the priests were to have the most essential parts of that service. Moses' brother Aaron was chosen as the first priest, and all his descendants were to have that office. In summary, as you can see in Figure 4.1, the Israelites were descended from Israel (Jacob). The Levites were descended from Israel's son Levi. This included Moses and Aaron. The priests were descended from Aaron. While only one generation separated Israel from Levi, many generations separated Levi from Aaron. Remember that hundreds of years elapsed between the end of *Genesis* and the other four books of Moses. All the Israelites would have been concerned with the book of *Leviticus*, but none as concerned as the priests and Levites themselves. Hence the name.

Like people today, the Israelites were concerned with personal health. Leviticus 11 to 15 provides instructions for food to be avoided and procedures to follow in the case of various infections. Though the specifics don't apply to us, it's not hard to see practical principles such as quarantining those with infectious diseases.

From chapter 16 to the end (chapter 27), attention is given to a variety of issues. Among these are the feasts, or religious festivals, that were to be part of the national culture. For example, the Israelites were to celebrate the deliverance from Egypt annually. The occasion was called Passover, because the angel of death had 'passed over' the Israelite homes and killed only the firstborn of Egypt's children. Every nation has its own set of holidays, fashioned from its history. This section of *Leviticus* is like an instruction booklet, describing for Israel the procedures and meaning of each special day.

In spite of its difficulty, *Leviticus* has diamonds to offer, and some of them are not far from the surface. When asked what was the greatest commandment in the Law of

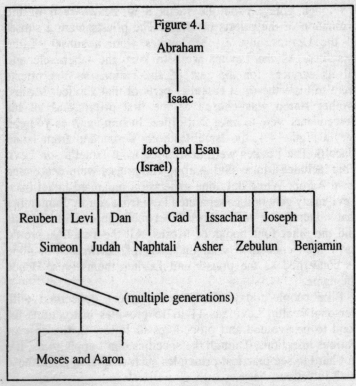

Figure 4.1

Abraham

Isaac

Jacob and Esau
(Israel)

Reuben | Levi | Dan | Gad | Issachar | Joseph

Simeon | Judah | Naphtali | Asher | Zebulun | Benjamin

(multiple generations)

Moses and Aaron

Moses, Jesus remembered something right in the middle of this book:

> "'Do not seek revenge or bear a grudge against one of your people, but love your neighbour as yourself. I am the LORD.'"

> Leviticus 19:18

There are no neon lights or advertising hoardings in the text to point the way to this gem. It's just there and He found it.

Nevertheless, we would be pressing our luck to make *Leviticus* the place to begin reading the Bible. It's best to regard it as an appendix to *Exodus*. When the details of the latter half of *Exodus* start interesting you, dive into *Leviticus* with both feet. Until then, you'd probably be happier just walking around it.

Numbers

Numbers tells of the journey of Israel from the foot of Mount Sinai (also called Mount Horeb) to the edge of the promised land. It was neither a quick trip nor a straight shot. About a year had elapsed since they first came out of Egypt. They spent most of that time erecting the tabernacle and establishing the priesthood. If it took them a year to assimilate the many details of Moses' regulations, you shouldn't berate yourself if you don't catch on right away.

Another of their activities was taking a census of the nation. This meant counting the males of fighting age, those twenty years old and upwards, by tribe. The total came to 603,550. God's promise of descendants to Abraham is thus shown to have staggering dimensions! These descendants had overcome the oppression of Egypt without lifting a spear, but the conquest of Canaan would be a different matter. In addition to helping with military strategy, the census would also help in the allocation of the promised land, once it was conquered. The tribes with larger populations would be assigned larger portions of the promised land.

A special census of the Levites and priests was also undertaken. They would be too busy with the tabernacle, its furnishings and sacrifices, and teaching the Law itself, to engage in battle. And for the sake of teaching, they would not have a territory of their own. Instead, their families would be dispersed throughout all the tribes of Israel to make Moses' teaching accessible to all Israelites. By the way, you have begun to see that the terms 'Law of Moses' and 'Law' can refer strictly to what Moses taught, as well as to the five books that contain that teaching.

By Numbers 10, all the preparations have been concluded and the fledgling nation and army have broken camp. Having had a year in the desert to get ready, they are on their way to glory. Unfortunately, the Israelites don't go far before the wheels start coming off. The internal squabbling that marred their march to Sinai prevails once again. They're tired of the food and sick of Moses telling everyone what to do. God is frustrated that His earlier miracles have failed to convince the people of His willingness and ability to provide for them in the midst of an otherwise hostile environment.

The climax to all this tension is reached in Numbers 13 and 14. At this point Moses commissions twelve spies, one from each tribe, to scout the promised land. They spend forty days at the task, covering it from one end to the other. They are favourably impressed with the land but scared to death of its current inhabitants. The spies said, 'We can't attack those people; they are stronger than we are.' A minority opinion by two of the spies was not enough to keep the nation from giving up all hope of winning the long promised land.

At the end of His rope, God decides to wait for the next generation of Israelites before attempting the invasion. That meant the current generation would spend the next forty years, one for each day they had spied out the land, wandering in the desert until they died and the new generation had taken their place. The few exceptions were those who had kept the right attitude.

Not much is told about the forty years of desert-wandering, except that the complaining never completely died out. But even though those years could have been considered wasted, God never failed to provide food and clothing. Another census was taken as the forty years drew to a close. Though the ranking of tribes by size changed, the nation's overall population was about the same. As the time to enter the land approached, Israel faced outlying nations in battle. In each case, Israel was granted victory. This built up their confidence as they approached Canaan.

From this summary you might get the idea that the book of *Numbers* is a straightforward action account. If so, it would be a false impression. The book's action is spread out and separated by lengthy stretches of census notes, procedural instructions for the march, and more of those detailed regulations we saw so much of in *Exodus* and *Leviticus*. Reader beware.

Deuteronomy

It would be hard to imagine a more fitting conclusion to Moses' books than *Deuteronomy*. It is the most personal of the five volumes. Here are the words Moses spoke to the nation as he was about to die and they were finally about to enter the promised land. He was eighty years old when he first told Pharaoh to let God's people go. Now he was 120. His approaching death was not so much because of diminished capacity: 'his eyes were not weak, nor his strength gone'. Rather, his own flaws determined that he should perish with the disobedient generation. Great as he was, Moses never came close to claiming perfection.

But even though he wasn't allowed to enter Canaan, he was allowed to view it from a mountaintop. The mere sight moved him so that he spoke with an eloquence to that rising generation that still lingers in the pages of this book. Like the respected old professor at a graduation ceremony, he seeks to ignite and direct the energy of a new generation, hoping against hope that it will outdo its elders.

In the first four chapters, Moses reviews some of the high points of the previous forty years. This includes the defeat of nations who rose against Israel, first told in *Numbers*. More often, though, he is forced to recount the low points of that period. This includes the episodes of complaining first recorded in *Exodus* and *Numbers*.

In Deuteronomy 5 Moses restates the Ten commandments. In the chapters that follow, he repeats many of the detailed laws first given in *Exodus, Leviticus*, and *Numbers*. Though much of his speech, whether of experiences or commandments, comes from the past, its purpose is to affect the future. He reminds the people that victory against the inhabitants of Canaan depends on Israel's faithfulness to God's instructions.

When you read about the inhabitants of the promised land, you'll see them generally called Canaanites. Sometimes they're named more specifically, and you'll see a string of names like Amorites, Hittites, Girgashites, Perizzites, and so on. Whatever their names, why should these people be forced to lose their land? Why should Israel be allowed to take it? Moses' argument was that these people were losing the land because of their wickedness in God's sight. Israel, on the other hand, was not gaining it because of any goodness of its own, but because of God's graciousness. And if Israel should fail to obey God, it, too, would one day be dispossessed. In other words, obeying the law he had proclaimed was not just a religious issue, but a matter of national survival.

The seeds of this idea are seen as far back as Genesis 15 when God tells Abraham (then Abram) that, though the land would be his, it would be a long time coming. God explained that the reason for the delay was that 'the sin of the Amorites has not yet reached its full measure'. In other words, the inhabitants of the land were not all that righteous, even back in Abraham's time. But God is patient and would suffer much before the disobedient would be required to forfeit the land. Therefore, the conditions which brought Israel to war with Canaan, and which were to bring Israel's ultimate victory in the contest, had been in the making for hundreds of years.

Moses was determined that this lesson should not be lost on the new nation. Like the Canaanites, they, too, would be shown patience by God. But if they misinterpreted that patience as indifference, they, too, would one day find themselves being driven from this piece of land. In Deuteronomy 27 and 28 Moses lays out in great detail the blessings that would attend their obedience and the curses that would attend their disobedience. Like a good parent, he kept bringing home the lessons of morality, even though he probably tired of it all.

Moses knew human nature too well to be totally optimistic. In fact, his prophecies at the end of the book darkly foreshadow the future of the nation. Undergirding all he says, however, is a conviction forged by years of trial that would have crushed a smaller man. That conviction was twofold: if Israel did right, God would reward, and if Israel did wrong, God would redeem. In that confidence he could rest his case and rest in peace. Thus concludes the final book of Moses.

In Review

This extended tour of the first section of the Bible reveals just how much there is to the Law of Moses. In order to be fair to its size and scope you may think that I was wrong to compare it merely to the U.S. Declaration of Independence and Constitution – that I should have thrown in the *Federalist* papers, George Washington's inaugural and farewell addresses, *Poor Richard's Almanac*, and the first forty years of the *Congressional Record*. You'd have a good point. The first five volumes of the Bible taken together are massive.

If you want a grip on early Bible history, you could read all of *Genesis* and the first half of *Exodus*, then skip *Leviticus*, hopscotch through *Numbers*, and, finally, skim *Deuteronomy*. This would give you a good understanding of how ancient Israel was conceived and birthed. On the other hand, taking one book at a time and seeking the treasures within it can be equally worthwhile. I've only mentioned the highlights of the story line. You'll find many fascinating curves in the road, and even a few enjoyable detours, as you read through yourself.

Don't forget to take a pencil along. You may want to make notes or marks to remind yourself where to return or where to do your own hopping. To mark a book and dog-ear its pages are aggressive acts that ought not to be engaged in lightly. But if the cause is good – and who can deny that understanding the Bible is a good cause? – then it ought to be encouraged. After all, the ultimate mark of respect for a book is that it is used. Marking your trail will help make this ancient literature as accessible to you as that produced in our own age.

Genesis, Exodus, Leviticus, Numbers and *Deuteronomy* provide a substantial foundation for the rest of the Bible. Like five great mountains, they stand majestically and invite the adventurous. Though they can be intimidating, it would take no longer than a day to scale any one of them, especially since you are now equipped with some knowledge of each.

Nevertheless, this is only one, and probably not the best, place to begin reading the Bible. Let's move on to the other sections, because there are many more doorways into the Bible than just these five.

5

The Books of History

If the books of Moses can be considered the cornerstone of
the Bible, then the next twelve books can be thought of as the
ground floor of the building. The historical record of ancient
Israel that began with *Genesis* to *Deuteronomy* is continued
with these twelve books. For this reason these twelve are
often called 'books of history'. While the Bible's first five
books brought Israel to the edge of the promised land, these
next twelve tell what happened once Israel took up residence
there. The history of the Israelites on that land included both
high points and low points. The highs were very high, and the
lows were very low.

As national histories go, these writings are quite candid.
They make no attempt to whitewash the failings of the
nation or its leaders. Fiascoes are given the same sort of
attention accorded to achievements. This refreshing historical
perspective is consistent with the rest of the Bible and with
ancient Israel's purpose: to call favourable attention not to
itself, but to the Creator. How He rewarded and redeemed
all the nations would be revealed in the rendering of an honest
history of the descendants of Abraham.

Size and Scope

If the books of Moses are like the continent of Africa, then
the books of history are like Asia – even bigger. The total
text of these twelve books runs almost a third longer than
the five books that precede them. All that was true of that
'Africa' – a vastness and a variety that can both intimidate

and invite – is also true of this 'Asia'. In some ways, even more true.

There is more diversity in size among these twelve books than there was among the first five. In the first five, the longest book was almost twice as long as the shortest. But in these twelve, the longest is almost ten times longer than the shortest. Even so, the longest book of history is considerably shorter than the book of Genesis (the longest of the books of Moses). We, therefore, have history that comes in a variety of portions, none of which is unbearably long.

Generally speaking, the style of these books of history follows that of Moses'. But since Moses' unique function was to 'lay down the law' for Israel, you won't find that particular element in these books. You will find, however, quotations from, paraphrases of, and allusions to that law throughout the books of history. That law was considered to be the governing force in the outworking of Israel's history.

The twelve books are arranged in chronological order. They begin with the time just after the death of Moses and continue for about a thousand years. Nevertheless, there are both overlaps and gaps in the historical record. *1* and *2 Chronicles*, for example, overlap the history recorded in the books of *Samuel* and *Kings*. As for gaps, we could wish to know more about what happened during the years between Israel's last king and the return of the exiles. Further, some periods receive more attention than others. We are told much more, for instance, about the time of Israel's kings than we are about the time of its judges. And we are told much more about the time of Israel's first kings than we are about its later ones.

This variation in the history points up once again that the Bible wasn't written by a single author as a single book. It was written in pieces, and the pieces were collected and put together. Each writer had a slightly different perspective and interest. Therefore, though we're always going forwards in our reading, we must be prepared to shift gears with each individual book we encounter.

Titles and Authors

The titles of the twelve books of history are generally taken from the leading, or at least a leading, figure of each book. Therefore, most of the titles are names of a person – *Joshua, Ruth, 1 and 2 Samuel, Ezra, Nehemiah*, and *Esther* – or names of groups of *persons – Judges, 1 and 2 Kings*. The only exception is *1 and 2 Chronicles*.

When the first five books of the Bible are viewed as a unit, they, too, are titled after a leading person: Moses. When viewed individually, the book titles we use are derived from the subject matter of each book. This titling is similar to that of *1* and *2 Chronicles*. All this helps show how the titles of Bible books are much less significant than titles of books produced in modern book publishing.

Let's compare the authorship of these twelve books of history to practices in modern book publishing. These books of history say little about who wrote them. Scholars speculate about the respective authors of each book, but only in two of them does the text itself seem to indicate an author. In *Ezra* and *Nehemiah* the authors write alternately in the third and first persons of the leading figure, indicating that Ezra and Nehemiah themselves are the respective authors.

As I stated in the first part of the guide, the normal apparatus of modern publishing that we are used to – authorship, title, date of publication, and table of contents – just aren't available for these individual books of the Bible. Instead, we are given a body of text which must speak for itself. Fortunately, these texts speak very well on this basis. The action they chronicle and the meaning they attach make the absence of titles and by-lines a minor disadvantage at most.

Joshua

Joshua succeeded Moses as leader of Israel. This book records what happened from the time of that succession until the death of Joshua. Therefore, the title refers to the fact that Joshua is the leading figure throughout the book.

For the most part, this book is a straightforward narrative. It does, however, get bogged down in the middle and I'll explain why.

The book opens some time after the death of Moses. God commissions Joshua to lead the Israelites across the Jordan River into Canaan, the promised land. This land was occupied by numerous city-states. The most well known of these was Jericho, a walled city just west of the Jordan.

Joshua prepares the nation for invasion and combat. He has specific instructions for two and a half of the twelve tribes of Israel. These two and a half tribes – Reuben, Gad, and half the tribe of Manasseh – had cut a deal with Moses. The deal allowed them to stake their claim on the east side of the Jordan River. The women and children were allowed to go ahead and stay there while the men had to cross the Jordan with the other nine and a half tribes and fight. Once the land west of the Jordan was secured, the two and a half tribes of soldiers would be allowed to return to their families on the east side of the river.

God arranged for this generation of Israelites to cross the Jordan River the same way the previous generation had crossed the Red Sea – on dry land. Remember that the generation that had been brought out of Egyptian slavery was required to wander in the wilderness for forty years. The two exceptions were Joshua and Caleb, the only two spies who had kept the right attitude about God's promise. After they crossed the Jordan, this new generation saw the manna cease to appear with the morning dew – the agricultural output of this fruitful land they were being given meant they would now enjoy a much more balanced diet.

Leading the way across the Jordan was the ark of the covenant, the central piece of furniture in the tabernacle they had constructed while in the desert. It was carried by the priest and symbolised the presence of God in the midst of the people.

With the walls of Jericho looking impregnable, the Israelites, led by their priests carrying the ark, simply circled it for six days. There was no fighting and the citizens of Jericho must have wondered about the meaning of such strange behaviour. On the seventh day, the Israelites let loose a war cry, and the walls came tumbling down. The Israelites easily won the battle for the city.

The next city of Canaan, Ai, proved a little harder to defeat. It's not that Ai was better defended that Jericho; it's that Israel had indulged in some behaviour that had weakened their relationship with God. Moses had warned clearly that, just as the Canaanites' behaviour had led to their losing their land, Israel's behaviour would affect their hold on the land, too. Joshua found the source of the problem, and Israel was restored to its winning ways.

As news of Israel's victories spread, the kings of Canaan became very frightened. The city of Gibeon finagled a treaty with Israel. Because of their deceit, the Israelites made them manual labourers and slaves – but the Gibeonites preferred that to dying in a losing cause.

Other cities made treaties with each other and fought Israel as groups. But even the greater force of these military alliances couldn't stem the tide of Israel's advance through the land. City after city fell. Chapter 12 lists thirty-one separate kings who were defeated.

The action and intrigue that marks the first half of the book comes to a screeching halt in chapters 13 to 20. It's here that the apportioning of the promised land is described in detail – excruciating detail. And all without reference to a map, which makes it wordier than it would otherwise be. Coupled with our ignorance of the landmarks of the time, this detail makes for extremely tedious reading. But in the closing chapters of *Joshua*, the stories with action return.

Particularly moving are Joshua's closing words to his people as he leaves the earth, echoing Moses' final words years before. Joshua reminds the Israelites that they have come to this land by a plan designed long ago in the heart of God. Their right to inherit the land is based upon their relationship to their ancestor Abraham. But their right to enjoy that land in peace is tied to how they lived – specifically, how they lived in accordance with the law handed down by Moses.

As Moses' speech was in *Deuteronomy*, Joshua's is sobering without being discouraging.

Judges

While Israel had indeed taken possession of the promised land, they had failed to drive out all the Canaanites completely. Within every tribal section of Israelite territory, there remained pockets of Canaanite resistance. God had warned that this might happen, that remaining Canaanites would be 'thorns in the sides' of the Israelites. These 'thorns' would be punishments and reminders to Israel that half-hearted obedience would not bring the full blessings that God had promised.

In addition to these internal threats, enemy nations surrounded Israel, too. All these threats would intensify or decrease, based on Israel's compliance with the law. When Israel was fulfilling its obligations before God, it enjoyed periods of peace. When it departed from the ways of the Lord, it experienced war and subjugation. This perspective – that history is an outworking of human behaviour and divine response – is a constant through all the Bible's writings. These twelve books simply highlight Israel as a case study in this view of history.

God had promised that when Israel did well, God would reward. He also promised that when Israel sinned, God would redeem. The primary way that God redeemed in those days was by raising up leaders, called judges or deliverers. These leaders were not selected to function as a prevailing authority like a king. Rather, they were raised up in times of crisis to accomplish certain purposes for God and the nation. Moses and Joshua fit this pattern. The book of *Judges* tells of the succession of leaders that followed in their steps. None of the crises were as great as the ones faced by Moses or even Joshua. Yet the work of the judges was important and contributed significantly to the wellbeing of Israel.

The history recorded in *Judges* covers several hundred years, beginning with the death of Joshua. The judges whose exploits are described are Othniel, Ehud, Shamgar, Deborah, Barak,

Gideon, Abimelech, Tola, Jair, Jephthah, Ibzan, Elon, Abdon and Samson. Except for one or two, these are not household names for us. Yet they were important and celebrated heroes to the people of their day.

Some of the judges are given no more than a sentence in the book. Gideon and Samson, on the other hand, are given several chapters apiece. The stories of the rest are told somewhere between these two extremes in length. The entire book is a string of these various episodes. The theme of the stories is Israel's recurring waywardness and God's recurring deliverance. Though Israel always brought misery on itself, God could only bear their misery so long before He would send them help. Just as God sent Moses when the Israelites cried from Egypt, so He continued to send deliverers whenever their descendants cried from the promised land.

The up-and-down graph of Israel's fortunes, however, shows an overall downward trend over the long haul. Towards the end of the book this phrase recurs: 'In those days Israel had no king; everyone did as he saw fit.' This description sets the stage for later books which describe the rise of a monarchy in Israel. As it is, *Judges* concludes with Israel behaving so corruptly that the reader of *Genesis* is reminded of the behaviour of Sodom and Gomorrah. This book's ending is far from 'happy ever after'.

Ruth

The short book of *Ruth* – shortest of all the historical books – provides a welcome respite from the harsh times described at the end of *Judges*. The title comes from the leading character of the vignette. Ruth and her mother-in-law, Naomi, are examples of how some of the best people can live and survive in the worst of times.

Naomi was married and had two sons. They lived in the time of the judges, though no specific judge is named in the book. For this reason, you could imagine this book as a four-chapter addendum to *Judges*. Famine had ravaged the promised land which God intended to 'flow with milk and honey'. Famine, like war, was a consequence of Israel's evil behaviour. The need for food forced Naomi's family to move to neighbouring Moab. While there, Naomi's two sons found wives: Ruth and Orpah.

Subsequently, Naomi's husband and two sons died. The one bit of good fortune that finally came Naomi's way is that the famine ended in Israel, allowing her to return to her homeland. Though a Moabite, Ruth had found something in Naomi that she didn't want to lose. She decided to move to Israel with her. Two widows in that day and age were about as economically disadvantaged as it was possible to be. However, through the shrewdness of Naomi, the devotion of Ruth, and some provisions of Mosaic law, a husband was found for Ruth. This husband was Boaz, a man of integrity and wealth who provided not only for the two widows, but also displayed how God can redeem the most hopeless of situations. Here is the happy ending that the book of *Judges* lacks.

If you've never read a whole book of the Bible in one sitting, this poignant story would make an excellent first selection. It is extremely short with a straightforward story line. Of all the Bible books we have reviewed so far, this one provides the simplest first step toward reading the Bible one book at a time. In less than fifteen minutes, you can complete your first book.

1 Samuel

As the book of *1 Samuel* opens, the period of the judges is still in effect. The judge of the day is the priest, Eli. He is old and his sons are corrupt. While serving in the tabernacle which now rests in the city of Shiloh, Eli saw a woman praying. The woman was Hannah, and she was praying for God to redeem her from infertility. She promised God that, if He should give her a child, she would devote that son to the service of the Lord. In that day, service to the Lord meant helping tend the tabernacle.

As God would have it, a son was born. Hannah named him Samuel. He began serving in the tabernacle at a very early age. In due time, he took Eli's place as the leading judge of Israel. All this takes up the first seven chapters of the book.

The most dramatic event to occur during this period was that the Israelites lost possession of the ark of the convenant. They were battling with the Philistines, a neighbouring power. Since putting the ark out front had worked when Joshua was leading the troops against Jericho, they thought they would try the same against the Philistines. The results were disastrous. The Philistines inflicted heavy casualties on the Israelites and seized the ark. The ark was eventually recovered – and in a rather exotic way – but the Israelites had been thoroughly humbled in defeat. They had been shown that even though the ark was of God's design, it was no talisman that guaranteed God's help. Only their attitude and behaviour could assure that.

In 1 Samuel 8, Israel asks Samuel to appoint them a king. The system of raising up judges for specific crises and missions made Israel look different from the surrounding nations. They wanted a king like all the other nations. God took this personally: a rejection of His kingship of Israel. Nevertheless, He instructed Samuel to grant their wishes and even selected the man who would be Israel's first human king – Saul.

1 Samuel 8 to 15 tells of Saul's early days, his successes and failures as king. Though he exhibited a courage which led Israel to victory against Israel's foes, he failed by either ignoring the direct commands of the Lord or only half-heartedly obeying them. Saul's waywardness so jeopardised Israel's wellbeing, that God was forced to look for another king to take his place.

1 Samuel 16 tells how Samuel notified David that he would be Israel's next king. David was still just a boy, yet the next chapter tells how he downed the Philistine giant, Goliath, with his slingshot. Actually, the sling in those days was no mere toy. The book of *Judges* describes 700 Israelite soldiers skilled enough with the device to 'sling a stone at a hair and not miss'. This was a weapon of military consequence. This fact doesn't diminish David's teenage exploit against Goliath, but simply paints it more accurately. From that day forward, David was a hero to Israel's army and its citizens.

Rather than rejoicing in David's victory, Saul felt threatened by it. David's favour with the people and with God made Saul feel insecure, and Saul began to devote all his efforts to preserving his throne. His own son Jonathan liked David and had no problem yielding his own claim to the throne. But Saul would have none of this humility and spent the remainder of his life looking more and more foolish. Finally, he was destroyed in battle by the Philistines. The book concludes on that sad note.

2 Samuel

Upon hearing of Saul's death, David grieved profusely and called the rest of the nation to do the same. The saddest part of Saul's threats against David was that David had no designs against Saul. Though David knew God had chosen him to replace Saul, David was content to wait until circumstances – Saul's abdication or death – invited his takeover. In the meantime, David was content to serve Saul as the first king of God's choice. Thus David was genuinely sad when Saul died, even though it meant he himself could now dwell in his homeland more securely.

With Saul gone, the twelve tribes of Israel began to unite around David. Prior to this time they had operated somewhat independently. During the time of the judges, God was ruler of the land. No centralised government ruled the nation. Worship was centralised through the tabernacle, but since the ark was seized from Shiloh, even that aspect of unification was absent.

One of the Canaanite strongholds that had long resisted Israelite force was the city of Jerusalem (alternately known as Jebus and Salem). One of David's many military victories as king was to capture this city. He chose to make it the capital of a united Israel. Upon taking the city, he decided to bring the ark of the covenant to it. This would solidify his reign both in political and religious terms.

David went on to defeat or take as allies the nations that surrounded Israel. Along the way he showed kindness to Saul's family, even though some of them initially resisted his reign in hopes that they themselves would inherit Saul's crown. Through it all, David was concerned with bringing glory to the God of Israel, fulfilling all that had been intended by the promises to Abraham and the law to Moses.

In 2 Samuel 11, in the middle of all these great deeds, David committed adultery, and then arranged a murder to cover it up. When no earthly power challenged him, God sent a prophet named Nathan to call the king to account. David showed the proper remorse. However, the rest of *2 Samuel* is taken up with the family problems David brought on himself by his evil.

First, the child born of adultery died after an illness. Then one of David's sons, Amnon, raped his sister. Another of David's sons, Absalom, quietly vowed revenge. Two years later Absalom had Amnon murdered, and, after that, he himself sought to usurp the throne from his father. There were prolonged battles, but David finally prevailed. The book closes with tributes to David's many exploits.

1 Kings

1 Kings could just as well be called *3 Samuel*, for it continues the narrative begun in *1* and *2 Samuel*. In fact, the books of *Samuel* and *Kings* comprise a four-volume history of the kings of Israel. Some older Bibles even title *1* and *2 Samuel* and *1* and *2 Kings* as *1* and *2* and *3* and *4 Kings*. Thus, the time after Moses is described in the book of *Joshua; Judges-Ruth* (two books) tells of the line of judges; and *Samuel-Kings* (four books) tells of the line of kings.

In the opening chapters of *1 Kings*, the throne of Israel is transferred from David to his son Solomon. The transition was threatened by another of David's sons. The challenge to Solomon's rule was turned back, however, and he ended up reigning for forty years. Because of David's military and political acumen, the borders of Israel were secure and its prosperity was substantial. In such an environment of peace, Solomon was free to pursue what had long been his father's dream: a permanent temple for the ark of the Lord to replace the portable tabernacle that had been built in the wilderness before Israel entered the promised land.

Solomon built a magnificent temple. Both the plans and provisions for it had been left by his father. This temple was the crowning achievement of Solomon's reign. When completed, it attracted attention from afar. Visiting dignitaries included the renowned queen of Sheba, a monarch of Africa. Upon seeing the sights in Jerusalem and meeting Solomon face to face she exclaimed, 'You have far exceeded the report I heard.'

1 Kings 4 gives some statistics about the administration of Solomon's kingdom. And 1 Kings 6 to 8 give details about the temple being built and dedicated. These chapters may seem a tedious departure from the action-oriented narrative that typifies the books of *Samuel-Kings*. But skim rather than skip them, for they offer a sense of the height of glory Israel had reached by the reign of Solomon. From the humble beginning of a single child named Isaac, the descendants of Abraham had risen to be a world power.

Unfortunately, Israel would not dwell long in these lofty heights. Abraham's legacy from the beginning was that there was one true God, no matter how much the other nations professed a galaxy of competing gods. And Moses had clearly warned the nation at its formation that devotion to this one God would be continually required of the people. Nevertheless, Solomon's heart became divided as he sought to accommodate the gods of Israel's allies. As a result of Solomon's divided heart, the entire nation became divided.

At the death of Solomon, Israel was split into northern and southern kingdoms. The southern kingdom was ruled by Solomon's son. It consisted of the tribes of Judah (the tribe from which David and Solomon came) and Benjamin and kept Jerusalem for its capital. The northern kingdom was made up of the remaining tribes who rebelled against Solomon. The northern kingdom was usually called Israel, while the southern kingdom was called Judah.

The remainder of *1 Kings* describes the fortunes of both of these kingdoms. The story continues chronologically, alternating between kingdoms.

All Moses' instructions for animal sacrifice and worship festivals centred on the ark of the covenant and its surroundings. Since David had fixed the ark's location in Jerusalem, the southern kingdom held the unifying force in Israel's national worship. Recognising this, the northern kingdom's first king established two golden calves at the borders, instructing citizens to worship there instead of going all the way to Jerusalem. These golden calves caused trouble in the same way that the golden calf at Mount Sinai in the book of *Exodus* had caused trouble. None of the northern kingdom's kings ever rectified this situation. Over the years, some of the northern kingdom's citizens, especially the Levites and priests, defected to Judah in order to pursue the ritual aspects of Moses' law.

2 Kings

1 Kings and *2 Kings* were orginally one book, and so the split between them is artificial. The story of the two kingdoms continues. Two prophets of great consequence ministered in the northern kingdom. The latter half of *1 Kings* tells of the exploits of Elijah, and the first part of *2 Kings* tells of his hand-picked successor, Elisha. These prophets often challenged the kings who were prone to self-serving behaviour. All Israelites were charged to love their neighbours. For the kings and subordinate leaders, this meant pursuing justice for all citizens.

The kings of the northern kingdom included Jeroboam, Nadab, Baasha, Elah, Zimri, Omri, Ahab (married to the infamous Jezebel), Ahaziah, Jehoram, Jehu, Jehoahaz, Jehoash, Jeroboam II, Zechariah, Shallum, Menahem, Pekahiah, Pekah and Hoshea. The lengths of their respective reigns varied considerably. The fortunes of the kingdom varied considerably under their reigns. While there were ups and downs, the overall decline was marked and certain from the beginning. Having been built upon the foundation of idolatrous worship (the golden calves), their ultimate demise was certain. By 2 Kings 17, the northern kingdom has been completely overrun by the mighty Assyria. Most authorities peg the date at 722 BC.

The kings of the southern kingdom included Rehoboam, Abijam, Asa, Jehoshaphat, Jehoram, Ahaziah, Athaliah, Jehoash, Amaziah, Uzziah, Jotham, Ahaz, Hezekiah, Manasseh, Amon, Josiah, Jehoahaz, Jehoiakim, Jehoiachin and Zedekiah. The southern kingdom took longer to fall. Scholars peg its demise at 586 BC, when Nebuchadnezzar of Babylon burned Jerusalem. He also took many exiles, particularly the educated ones, to Babylon to serve him there.

Centuries before, Moses had warned the Israelites that they, too, might be driven from this land as the Canaanites had been. Now it was happening, just as Moses had feared. Israel had enjoyed many years on the land, some of them quite glorious. But in the end, their own sins – their failure to execute justice among themselves and towards others, and their worship of other gods – had caused them to forfeit their right to the land. They found themselves exiled from the very land God had promised them.

When the Babylonians captured Israel's king, they killed his sons before his eyes . . . and then put out his own eyes and brought him in chains to Babylon. This epitomised the shame and degradation which had come upon the descendants of Abraham. Better days are ahead, but we'll have to read past *2 Kings* to find them.

1 Chronicles

The books of *Chronicles* are not a continuation of the history of Israel, but rather a repeat of it. To put it simply: *Chronicles* is a condensed version of *Samuel-Kings*. This doesn't mean *Chronicles* is an exact miniature of *Samuel-Kings*. Its structure and contents are at times very different.

The first nine chapters of *1 Chronicles* are basically genealogy. You will only enjoy reading this if you enjoy curling up with phone books. The narrative portion begins in 1 Chronicles 10 with the story of King Saul dying while battling against the Philistines. The rest of *1 Chronicles* deals with David's kingdom. There is considerably more focus on the ark of the covenant, how it was set up, and how it served in Jerusalem. This book tells less of David's foreign exploits and family problems and more about the music and singing he established for the priesthood. Interspersed throughout the narrative are lists of Levites and priests who had responsibilities for various worship activities.

This book also dwells on the provisions David made for the temple before his death. It includes prayers, songs of thanksgiving, and words of dedication that he composed for the occasion. It also tells how he commissioned Solomon for the task of building the temple.

2 Chronicles

2 Chronicles begins with Solomon taking the throne. The first nine chapters cover his reign, repeating information from *Samuel-Kings* and adding details of its own. The rest of the book dwells entirely on the affairs of the southern kingdom. The northern kingdom is mentioned only in passing. As with *Samuel-Kings*, the historical record ends with destruction at the hands of Babylon.

Chronicles' focus on the southern kingdom has to do with its concern for proper temple worship and kingly rule from Jerusalem. Proper temple worship meant priests who could prove their lineage from the tribe of Levi and from Aaron and who served at the true temple that David had established in Jerusalem. Proper kingly rule meant having a king who was a descendant of David – as all the kings of the southern kingdom were. *Samuel-Kings* mentions these issues, but *Chronicles* emphasises them.

Genealogies and lists, which would help trace the lineage of potential priests and kings, are sprinkled throughout the two books of *Chronicles*. As a result, reading *Chronicles* will require more skipping and skimming than will reading *Samuel-Kings*. Putting it another way the percentage of straight storytelling is much closer to 100 per cent in *Samuel-Kings* than in *Chronicles*.

Ezra

The exile first of the Israelites in the Northern Kingdom and then of those in the Southern Kingdom resulted in the dispersion of the Jews into every corner of the world. Historians have referred to these scattered Jews as the Diaspora. They began meeting together in various locations, and the groups that met were called 'synagogues' (meaning assembly). The buildings in which they met came to be called 'synagogues' as well. The idea of 'synagogue' arose not out of the law of Moses, but out of the needs of the Diaspora for mutual encouragement.

The term 'Jew' was derived from the word 'Judah'. It has come to refer to any descendant of Abraham. Therefore, whether the Bible speaks of Hebrews, Israelites, or Jews, it has the same people in view. Generally speaking, 'Hebrew' was used from the time of Abraham to Moses, 'Israelite' was used from the time of Moses to the exile, and 'Jew' was used after the exile. Even so, use of the terms is not always precise.

About seventy years after the destruction of Jerusalem, Jews began returning to their holy city. The book of *Ezra* describes the exiles' return. By this time, Babylon had been replaced by Media-Persia as a world power. Permission for the return was granted by the friendly edict of the Persian king. Ezra was a priest who led a contingent of Jews to their homeland. The second chapter is taken up with a detailed census of those who returned.

The otherwise dry census numbers are made poignant if you notice that they are only fractions of the numbers of people that came out of Egypt. The greatest value of the census numbers in the Bible lies in what they say when you compare them with one another. And while the raw numbers make for tiresome reading, the comparison of them tells a fascinating story. Abraham was promised innumerable descendants. He had one. From that one came two, and from those two, twelve. From the twelve came some seventy who went down to Egypt. By the time of Moses centuries later, there were hundreds of thousands. And now in the time of Ezra, only a remnant of those great numbers returned to the land. There were countless others dispersed throughout the world, to be sure. Thus, the little groups returning to the promised land spoke loudly of how a faithful God deals with His faithless people.

Much of *Ezra* deals with temple worship and its responsibilities, just as *Chronicles* had. For this reason, the author may have been the same. Ezra's interest is in teaching the details of the law of Moses, so that Jews can reinstitute the practices on the promised and that Moses had envisioned.

Nehemiah

The story of Nehemiah also takes place in the middle of repatriating the land of Israel. Nehemiah's particular concern was the security of Jerusalem itself. The city was constantly raided by various marauders. Nehemiah returned from exile specifically to help. Upon viewing the city firsthand, he saw that the city walls needed to be rebuilt. He organised the people and completed the task in fifty-five days.

While Ezra's role was that of priest, Nehemiah's was that of governor. In principle, both followed in the pattern of Israel's prior leaders: Moses, Joshua, the judges, and the kings. The nation was now no more than a stump of the glorious tree it had once been. Gone were the glory of kings, but various governors and priests would lead the people and deal with the foreign powers to whom some form of subservience was always required – now the Persians, later the Greeks, and later still the Romans.

There is some repetition between *Ezra* and *Nehemiah*. For example, the census of returning exiles in Ezra 2 is found also in Nehemiah 7. The books dovetail in others ways, too. Each deals with the same general historical period and tells from different perspectives how a chastened nation sought a measure of reconstruction. Ezra viewed the rebuilding as a priest, charged with teaching what the law of Moses required and what the books of history had revealed. Nehemiah viewed it as a governor, charged with enforcing that law while dealing with foreign powers both friendly and hostile. *Ezra-Nehemiah* makes a distinctive pair of books, together recording the rebuilding of Jerusalem after the exile.

Esther

While *Ezra-Nehemiah* deal with events in Jerusalem, *Esther* deals with events far away. As *Ruth* was a vignette sketched in the period of the judges, so *Esther* is a vignette sketched in the time of the exile. As one of the exiles, Esther finds herself in the service of the king of Persia. She lost her mother and father and was raised by her older cousin Mordecai. The opening chapter describes how the queen of Persia lost her throne by embarrassing the king with her defiance. Beautiful young women were rounded up, from whom the king might pick a new queen. Esther found herself among them.

Mordecai told Esther not to reveal that she was a Jew. After a lengthy selection process, Esther was chosen to be the new queen. About this same time, a young prince named Haman rose rapidly in the service of the king. He was ambitious and proud. Because the Jews worshipped the one true God, Haman couldn't get the same kind of adulation from them as he could from the rest of the king's subjects. As a result, he decided to annihilate all the Jews, without realising that the queen herself was one.

Through a fascinating sequence of events, Haman's rampage against the Jews backfires. Esther retains the favour of the king, even when it is revealed that she's Jewish. Mordecai is promoted to vice-regent of the country, and Haman dies along with most of his family. The book highlights God's ability to take care of His people, even when they are far away from the promised land. Though *Esther* is twice as long as *Ruth*, it's still short – no longer than a short story in a magazine. It's another excellent first step in reading the Bible book by book.

Looking Back

These twelve books of history combine to finish the story that Moses began. As Moses described how ancient Israel was formed, these books describe how it fared. Israel's beginning was filled with hope and promise. At the end, it had become a shadow of its former self: a humble remnant of a once great power. Out of that remnant would come the historical events of the New Testament. But until then, the historical record of the Scripture would be closed. The books of poetry and prophecy don't extend the historical line of the Old Testament – they fill in the existing one.

The central focus of the twelve books of history is the kingdom of Israel. The first three books – *Joshua, Judges*, and *Ruth* – tell of pre-kingdom days. The next six books – two each of *Samuel Kings*, and *Chronicles* – tell of kingdom days. And the last three – *Ezra, Nehemiah*, and *Esther* – tell of post-kingdom days. The middle six books take up much more than half of the total pages involved. For even the shortest of the kingdom books is longer than any of the pre-kingdom or post-kingdom books. Thus, the bulk of the material in the historical books tells about Israel's kings. The days of Joshua and then the judges constitute a prelude, and the days of the return from exile a postlude. Not all of the kings are given equal coverage. Israel's first three kings – Saul, David, and Solomon – are covered extensively. The stories of their reigns take up more than half of the six books of *Samuel, Kings*, and *Chronicles*.

The first seventeen books of the Bible – the books of Moses plus the books of history – provide a history of ancient Israel from its founding down to about 400 BC. Like any history book (or series of history books), the records focus more attention on some time periods than others. I'm not trying to make a statement about *why* the Bible documents some times more than others – only that it does. And I'm wanting you to have a sense of the contours of that history so that when you read an individual book, you'll have a sense of where it fits in the whole.

Let's look at this history in terms of the leaders of ancient Israel. *Genesis* gives the background of the nation: how it came to be. *Exodus* to *Esther* tell of its leaders beginning with Moses, then Joshua, then a succession of judges, then a succession of kings, and finally – after its exile and partial return – through various governors and foreign dominations.

The next two sections of books – poetry and prophecy – elaborate on certain aspects of the history we have seen. Further, the books of poetry and prophecy give more insight into the workings of that history. These books confirm and amplify the theme of all the books we have discussed so far: that history is the sum total not just of humanity's actions, but of God's as well.

6

The Books of Poetry

The next five books in the Bible – *Job, Psalms, Proverbs, Ecclesiastes*, and *Song of Songs* – are called books of poetry. If the previous two sections of books can be compared to Africa and Asia, then this section can be likened to Australia. For one thing, this section of books is much smaller than either of the first two sections. For another, while the first two sections had a close connection between them, this one stands independently. And lastly, this section has ports on all sides – that is, it is accessible from any direction. These characteristics will become clearer as this chapter unfolds.

The Nature of Hebrew Poetry

Not all English poetry rhymes. This is fortunate because it helps us appreciate Hebrew poetry . . . none of which rhymes. Hebrew poetry is picturesque and vivid. It's filled with concrete images and emotion-evoking thoughts. It touches the soul . . . making us think and feel. Though it's missing rhyme, it's missing nothing else that is characteristic of good poetry.

The absence of rhyme is actually beneficial. Most of the people who read the poetry of the Bible are reading it in some language other than Hebrew. It's hard enough to translate from one language to another. To find a foreign word that not only matches the meaning of the original, but also the sound, is terribly difficult. Inevitably, sacrifices have to be made in the precision of the word chosen. The absence of rhyme in the Hebrew scheme leaves translators free to choose the word with meaning closest to that of the original – regardless of its sound. This leaves us, then, with English translations for the poetry which is as faithful to the original words as the prose. Whatever other genius may lie in Hebrew poetry, this 'transportability' to other languages is worthy of appreciation.

There is a rhythm or cadence to Hebrew poetry which is lost to some degree in the translation. But what does come through is noticeable . . . and powerful. Notice, for example, the rhythm in these opening lines of the first psalm:

> Blessed is the man
>   who does not walk in the counsel of the wicked
> or stand in the way of sinners
>   or sit in the seat of mockers.

> Psalm 1:1

The poet is drawing us a picture of a person who is blessed. There are three brushstrokes, each elaborating on the same point. Each line, therefore, repeats and intensifies the image. Note also the walk-stand-sit progression. Now for the next two lines:

> But his delight is in the law of the LORD,
>   and on his law he meditates day and night.

> Psalm 1:2

Now the picture shifts to the man's inward activities. He 'delights' in the law of the Lord. The law of the Lord can be thought of as the law laid down by Moses, or, more likely, the sum total of the man's understanding of what the Lord expects of us. The next line repeats and intensifies the idea of delight in the law: he 'meditates' on it all the time. And now the next line:

> He is like a tree planted by streams of water,
>   which yields its fruit in season

and whose leaf does not wither.
Whatever he does prospers.

Psalm 1:3

The poet brings in the image of a tree. The next line has us focusing on the fruit that comes forth at the right time. The line after that has us noticing the leaves which fail to wither because of the nearby streams. The implication is that the 'streams' are the thought processes he is continually engaged in: meditating upon and delighting in the law of the Lord. The final line in this segment brings us directly back to the man. He prospers in whatever he does. That is, he's fruitful like the tree – productive. The psalm concludes by painting a contrasting picture of shadowy figures of the wicked, sinners, and mockers who were mentioned in the opening lines:

Not so the wicked!
    They are like chaff
    that the wind blows away.
Therefore the wicked will not stand in the judgment,
    nor sinners in the assembly of the righteous.

For the LORD watches over the way of the righteous,
    but the way of the wicked will perish.

Psalm 1:4–6

The wicked are as different from the righteous as chaff is from a tree. A tree firmly planted can withstand the wind, but chaff is blown away. This contrast balances out the psalm and gives it a sense of symmetry. This results in a vivid word picture for the reader. Thus, the image in the psalmist's mind is effectively communicated to the reader's mind. Dwelt on long enough, the picture will reproduce the psalmist's emotions in the heart of the reader. Read the poetry in the Bible with an eye for matching ideas instead of sounds, and you'll quickly get to the heart of the poet's message. The method of constant comparison and contrast, repeated and intensified, is the essence of Hebrew poetic structure. It's sometimes called parallelism.

Reading this poetry is enormously satisfying, but it must be read slowly. Remember that I urged you to read all the ancient literature of the Bible more slowly than you normally read. And when you come to its poetry, slow down even more. Your patience will be rewarded with word pictures which become increasingly focused and meaningful. The poetic structure of parallelism guarantees emphasis, elaboration, comparison, or contrast of every important idea in the poem.

Wisdom Literature

The books of poetry aren't just a departure in style from the previous books. They're a departure in subject matter, too. While history has been the primary focus to this point, wisdom takes centre stage with these five books. For this reason, the books of poetry are often called the 'wisdom literature' of the Bible.

These books of wisdom act as commentary on the history of Israel. Over the years, the Israelites accumulated significant insights about the human experience. First, they had direct communications from the Creator. The most important of these were preserved in the Scriptures. Generation after generation had opportunity to mull these over. Much of the wisdom literature is a result of Israel's extended meditation upon God's ideas. Thus, the wisdom literature expresses in poetic form the distilled wisdom of a nation with unique access to the mind of God.

This wisdom was much more than a rephrasing of statements God had made, however. It was wisdom forged on the anvil of experience. You could read books about boxing and then wax poetic about the sport. But if, before you waxed poetic, you spent a considerable amount of time in the ring working out those principles you read, your poetic expressions would be immeasurably truer and more practical. Thus, the wisdom literature of the Bible is not pie-in-the-sky morality. Rather, it's reality-based inspiration.

Another way of putting it is that these books of poetry carry the lessons learned from the books of history. For example, the book of *Joshua* opens with God's commission to Joshua as he was about to lead the nation into the promised land. Part of God's charge to Joshua was:

> Do not let this Book of the Law depart from your mouth; meditate on it day and night, so that you may be careful to do everything written in it. Then you will be prosperous and successful.

> Joshua 1:8

With Psalm 1 fresh in your mind, you should have no trouble seeing the connection between this passage from *Joshua* and that one. It's possible that these words were the psalmist's primary inspiration. The idea is that the person who is constantly thinking about what God wants prospers, or has success, in his or her activities. The contrasting imagery of a tree versus chaff calls to mind Israel's own experience on the promised land: a tree has roots to withstand the wind, while the chaff is simply blown away. Israel stayed rooted for a while in the promised land but was eventually blown away in the Babylonian exile. Israel's experience has proven that God's words to Joshua were profound and prophetic . . . and worthy of magnifying with a poetic expression.

The books of poetry are thus filled with allusions to words, people, events, and locations described in earlier books of the Bible. The more of the Bible you read, the more of these connections you'll be able to make and appreciate. Equally beneficial, however, is the fact that you don't have to have read any of the other Bible books in order to be able to begin appreciating the wisdom books. They stand on their own and offer considerable reading pleasure without a knowledge of the rest of the Bible. In fact, these books are one of the best places to begin your Bible reading – in many ways they are a better starting place than most of the books we have covered so far.

Psalm 23, for instance, has been a treasure to many readers over many centuries. It is short, and many people know it by heart. If you were introducing someone to the Bible who'd never had any previous exposure to the book, you could open to Psalm 23, and the reader could appreciate this brief poem without having read any other part of the Bible. Later on, this novice Bible reader might come across the passage in Genesis which reads:

> "May the God before whom my fathers
>   Abraham and Isaac walked,
> the God who has been my shepherd
>   all my life to this day,
> the Angel who has delivered me
>   from all harm . . ."
>   Genesis 48:15–16

These are some of the words Jacob spoke near the end of his life. They are poetic, and several threads of Psalm 23 can be seen in them: 'God is my shepherd', 'all my life', 'walk', 'deliver from evil'. It's possible that these very words provided the particular inspiration for this Psalm. Jacob's descendant, David, penned Psalm 23 centuries later as he tended his father's sheep. I read Psalm 23 with enjoyment for years before I ever saw this particular connection with Genesis. But my appreciation has been enriched beyond measure since that time. Thus, the wisdom literature is a good place to start reading the Bible because it makes sense even to Bible newcomers. But it's also a good place for Bible old-timers because these books only deepen the sense and the meaning.

The Relation of the Books to Each Other

These books of poetry – *Job, Psalms, Proverbs, Ecclesiastes* and *Song of Songs* – not only stand independent from the other Bible books, they also stand independent of each other. There is no historical progression from book to book as there was with *Genesis* to *Deuteronomy* and continuing with *Joshua* to *Esther*. None of the poetry books builds its understanding on the one that came before it.

There is, however, a faint chronological sequence to the

books. The first book deals with Job, a man considered to have lived in the time of the book of *Genesis*. Next come the *Psalms*, which are associated primarily with David who of course, lived in the time of the kings. The next three books – *Proverbs, Ecclesiastes* and *Song of Songs* – are all associated with Solomon, the son of David. These three men are only general reference points, for there are psalms and proverbs associated with other people who lived much later. So the historical sequence is a background issue.

While all five books bear the general mark of poetry, they are by no means identical to each other. Both style and subject matter vary with each book. The books are almost as different from each other as the group is from all the books that preceded them. Each is a unique lyrical expression of the wisdom God gave to ancient Israel.

Job

One of the most profound and challenging questions that has ever confronted the human mind is, 'Why do bad things happen to good people?' Whenever this question arises, the book of *Job* is sooner or later brought into the discussion. No piece of literature, ancient or modern, deals more directly and effectively with this question than the book of *Job*. Its effectiveness lies in the fact that it doesn't answer the question with a pat answer. Rather, it involves the reader in a wrestling match of thought between a small group of characters who themselves struggle with the question.

The book of *Job* reads like the script for a play. The central characters are Job, three of his friends, a bystander and God. The supporting cast includes Job's a wife and children, the angels and Satan as chief of the angels. The first two chapters are prose, the last chapter is prose, and the intervening thirty-nine chapters consist of poetic dialogue between the central characters. If you picture the dialogue taking place on a stage, or around a campfire, you'll have a good framework for digesting the words.

The opening prose section gives the setting. Job is a

successful man. He owns abundant livestock (better than a limitless credit card in the economy of those times), and has ten happy children. His success is attributed to his spiritual integrity, his 'fear of God'. By the way, whenever the Bible speaks of fearing God, it isn't talking about cowering or being terrorised – it's talking about reverential awe. Job's success in life is attributed to his reverential awe of his Maker.

Satan (the name means 'adversary') challenges God about this before all the other angels in heaven. Satan contends that Job only fears God for the rewards that it brings him. Take those away, says the challenger, and Job will lose his morality fast. God accepts the challenge, and Job encounters a series of misfortunes which rob him of all his prosperity and all his children. When Job refuses to curse God, Satan ups the ante and suggests removing Job's health. But even when Job is covered from head to foot with sore boils, he still refuses to abandon his integrity. At this point, the dialogue begins in chapter three.

Three of Job's friends come to comfort him. No one says a word for a week, and then Job bemoans his condition. One of his friends responds, and then Job speaks again. Another friend responds, and then Job speaks again. So the conversation goes, alternating between Job and one of his friends. Although the chapter divisions were added centuries after the book was written, they fit the scheme of speech. Each person speaks for a chapter or two at a time.

Job's friends are sympathetic to his plight but grow more insistent that he must own up to whatever wrong he had done to bring on the catastrophe. Job contends that his lifestyle has been consistent, that this change in circumstances has not been the result of a change in his morals. So steadfast is Job on this point that his friends finally give up speaking to him. A bystander who has been listening decides to enter the fray. He takes a different tack, and Job does not interrupt him. After a while, God Himself begins to speak to Job, calling him to account. Job has nothing to say, except to say that he's sorry he ever said anything in the first place.

God then defends Job to his friends, and, once Job prays

for them, God restores double all Job's livestock. Job even receives another ten children. The question as to why the righteous suffer is never answered directly, which is the answer. The point is that the righteous indeed sometimes suffer in this life, for reasons that cannot be immediately explained or understood. Job was right that he had done nothing to bring on the disaster. The reason for the disaster was Satan's challenge, which occurred in heaven – a realm beyond the awareness of Job and his friends. Job was innocent of wrongdoing, but he did err by joining in the chorus for a simple explanation.

Job is one of the most heroic figures in all of literature. Although the modern connotation attached to Job's name is that of haplessness and unending misfortune, a reading of the book reveals that he was greatly blessed before his trial, which lasted no more than weeks or months, and even more greatly blessed after it. And he lived for over one hundred years. That he withstood the challenges of angelic contempt and power is a moving expression of the majesty of human morality. You probably won't want to make this the first book of the Bible you choose to read, but neither will you want to make it your last.

Psalms

If the Bible is a collection of writings, then *Psalms* is the collection within the collection. And while the Bible has sixty-six pieces, *Psalms* has 150. The shortest psalm is just two verses:

> Praise the LORD, all you nations;
>   extol him, all you peoples.
> For great is his love towards us,
>   and the faithfulness of the LORD endures for ever.
>
> Praise the LORD.

Psalm 117

(Note, by the way, the parallelism of 'praise' and 'extol', 'the

LORD' and 'him', 'all you nations' and 'all you peoples'. You can also see parallels in the next two lines and the rounding out of the whole with the final, 'Praise the Lord'.)

The longest psalm is just two psalms later, Psalm 119. It is also the longest chapter in the Bible, longer than some whole Bible books – such as *Obadiah, Philemon* and *Jude* – which are no more than a chapter long themselves. Thus, the psalms range in length from very short to very long.

Most psalms, however, fall between five and fifteen verses. They are, therefore, long enough to provoke substantial thought, but not so long that they discourage the casual reader.

The 150 psalms are organised into five 'books' as follows:

Book I	Psalms 1 to 41 (41 psalms total)
Book II	Psalms 42 to 72 (31 psalms total)
Book III	Psalms 73 to 89 (17 psalms total)
Book IV	Psalms 90 to 106 (17 psalms total)
Book V	Psalms 107 to 150 (44 psalms total)
	for a total of 150 psalms

It appears that this collection was begun as something of a hymn-book for temple worship in Jerusalem. Littered throughout the collection are the words *selah, maskil*, and *mikhtam*, which all seem to function as the words *forte* or *pianissimo* do on a piece of music. That is, they give direction to those who would speak or chant these psalms in public worship. Some of the psalms make reference to a choir director before the words of the psalm actually begin. The book of *Chronicles* explains the elaborate system of music and singing that David established for the temple. Although the meaning of many of these individual expressions are lost to us, their presence in the collection seems to fit with the system *Chronicles* describes.

Though scholars find some logic in the sequence of certain psalms, there is no apparent overall sequence which would guide you from the first psalm to the last. They appear almost as a random collection. Therefore, reading them means approaching each one individually. This is good news for the browser. You won't have cheated yourself if you skip through, looking for something appealing.

I've already shown you Psalms 1 and 117. You've probably already read or heard Psalm 23. Using one of those as a starting point, you can branch out and see what you find.

Be prepared for the widest possible range of emotional tones in these poems. Though the three psalms I just mentioned are upbeat, you also find some cries of despair. In fact, Psalm 22 begins, 'My God, my God, why have you forsaken me?' Jesus repeated these words as He hung from the cross. Though the question was written centuries before His humiliating death, Jesus thought they fit His situation perfectly. You may likewise find words that fit your varying circumstances and moods. Thoughts of doubt, despair, and uncertainty coexist with thoughts of faith, hope, and unwavering conviction. While the subject of *Psalms* is God, it is an altogether human book.

Many of the psalms carry a heading, such as 'A Psalm of David'. This may mean that David himself wrote the psalm, or it may mean that it was written in the style of David, or even under the authority of David. What is certain is that David brought this art form we call a psalm to prominence in the Hebrew culture. His expressive personality and devotion to the God of Israel are what give the pieces of this collection their distinctiveness. That many of the psalms were written by David's contemporaries and even by the generations after him bear witness to the impact of his artistry and faith.

Some psalms give even more than a reference to a name – they refer to an event. For example, Psalm 51 is prefaced with a phrase about the adultery and murder episodes of David's life. The psalm is about remorse and repentance, and so the little preface makes perfect sense. Most of the psalms, however, lack any such explanation, so we must take them at face value. Clearly, the face value of these psalms is enormous, according to generations of readers.

The numbers which differentiate the psalms are only a fraction less informative than the single-word titles given to the books of the Bible. In both cases we have tags added to pieces of literature for the purpose of identification by later readers and scholars – not by the original authors. The book of *Psalms*, as a microcosm of the Bible, instructs us how to approach the Bible. That is, sample the pieces and see what they say. Then the title tag – whether it's a name or number – will become invested with meaning for you. Until you do that reading, it's just a number or a name.

Because you will probably find psalms that are particularly enjoyable and meaningful, you will probably want to keep a supply of bookmarks to mark them. Or you may make a list. Or you may dog-ear the pages, or even mark the pages with your pencil. Getting this physical with a book isn't always necessary, but the Bible is so much bigger than any ordinary book that extraordinary measures are in order. It can be like a vast cave, and if you don't leave markers to show where you've been, the vastness can keep overwhelming you. How do you cover a continent like Australia and not get lost in the outback? Leave a trail wherever you go.

Proverbs

Proverbs is another major collection within the Bible. Unfortunately, the proverbs are not laid out as clearly as the psalms. Chapter divisions fit the framework of the psalms very well: each psalm constitutes a chapter. *Proverbs* are so much shorter, though, that you can't make chapters out of them. Further, some of the proverbs are strung together in a meaningful sequence. Others are independent of each other but packed together just the same. Let me illustrate.

Here is a portion of the first chapter of *Proverbs*:

> Listen, my son, to your father's instruction
>   and do not forsake your mother's teaching.
> They will be a garland to grace your head
>   and a chain to adorn your neck.
>
> My son, if sinners entice you,
>   do not give in to them.
> If they say, 'Come along with us;

> let's lie in wait for someone's blood,
> let's waylay some harmless soul . . .'
>
> Proverbs 1:8–11

You can see that these lines are continually building and going somewhere. The lines continue for another eight verses before they reach a climax.

Contrast those lines with these from a later chapter:

> Better a dry crust with peace and quiet
> than a house full of feasting, with strife.
>
> A wise servant will rule over a disgraceful son,
> and will share the inheritance as one of the brothers.
> The crucible for silver and the furnace for gold,
> but the LORD tests the heart.
>
> A wicked man listens to evil lips;
> a liar pays attention to a malicious tongue.
>
> Proverbs 17:1–4

Here we see individual proverbs, rather than an extended one as before. Each proverb must be digested individually. Thus, these four verses read *much more slowly* than the previous four verses. But there was no warning in the text, no sign in the chapter-verse apparatus to warn us that something different was coming.

Moreover, there may indeed be a connection between these proverbs that is not immediately apparent. More reflective reading might reveal a progression of thought that we otherwise might miss. The point is that while chapter divisions help us sort out the collection of 150 psalms, they do little to help us negotiate these hundreds of proverbs.

Imaginereadingaparagraphofsentencesthatwerepackedtogetherwithnospacestomakeclearwhenonewordorsentencewasendingandanotherwasstarting. You could read such a paragraph, but it would take you a little extra time to unpack the words. Similarly, the proverbs require some unpacking when you read them. Allow for that time, and you will probably find immense pleasure in them.

You may have noticed the recurring parallelism in the proverbs above. Here's another:

> A gentle answer turns away wrath,
> but a harsh word stirs up anger.
>   Proverbs 15:1

'Wrath' matches with 'anger', while 'gentle' contrasts with 'harsh', and 'turns away' correspondingly contrasts with 'stirs up'. Balance and symmetry, but not in a uniform fashion. The variations are endless. It may be point-point, or point-counterpoint, or point-point-point, and so on. Hebrew maxims don't carry the rhyme of 'A stitch in time saves nine', but they do carry the balanced punch of 'A penny saved is a penny earned'.

The opening chapters of *Proverbs* carry the extended variety. It's mostly one-liners from chapter 10 on. But there are exceptions all along the way, so you'd better keep your eyes open. The easiest initiation into this genre is to sit down and go over just one chapter. If you don't get at least one chuckle and one wince out of that much, I'll be surprised.

Ecclesiastes

If *Job* reads like a play, and *Psalms* reads like poems, and *Proverbs* reads like a book of maxims, then *Ecclesiastes* reads like an essay. The subject is the vanity of life. The book approaches in a different way the same question that *Job* approaches. That is, if this universe is governed by a moral God, why doesn't everything make sense?

If nothing in life made sense, we'd never ask the question. It's precisely because so much in life makes sense, that we're bothered by the parts that don't. *Ecclesiastes* alternates between prose and poetry so smoothly that you don't always realise when you're shifting gears. The book begins with 'Meaningless! Meaningless!' When an author begins like this you have to wonder where she or he is going. The conclusion of the book is that, regardless of any apparent meaninglessness, fearing God and keeping His commandments is the wisest course of action. Though some of its statements and its occasionally cynical tone put it at variance with some other Bible books, *Ecclesiastes'* conclusion is right in line with the thrust of all Bible writing.

Ecclesiastes is the first book of the Bible that I ever read from beginning to end. Though I had no interest in religious matters at the time, the book thoroughly impressed me. I felt that the writer really understood human consciousness, particularly the disappointments that life often brings. I still find this essay fascinating, and it continues to yield new insight every time I read it. This is the book that contains the passage:

> There is a time for everything,
> and a season for every activity under heaven:
>
> a time to be born and a time to die,
> a time to plant and a time to uproot,
> a time to kill and a time to heal,
> a time to tear down and a time to build . . .
> Ecclesiastes 3:1–3

These words have found their way even into twentieth-century popular music. Though they were penned thousands of years ago, they still resonate in human minds and hearts. These words obviously express a voice of wisdom, and that voice can be heard throughout the essay.

Ostensibly, the author of the piece is Solomon. The name is never explicitly used, but the author refers to himself as 'the son of David' and 'king in Jerusalem'. Of course, Solomon was described in *Samuel-Kings* and again in *Chronicles* as possessing enormous wisdom. You can easily read this book in one sitting, but you'll probably want to go back and take a section at a time to extract some of its many treasures.

Song of Songs

In terms of style, the *Song of Songs* could be titled Psalm 151. It continues in that tradition of emotionally expressive and picturesque poetry. It is lengthy as psalms go (eight

chapters-worth). And it does have a more complex voicing
than most psalms: instead of a single speaker there is a bride,
bridegroom and chorus who alternately speak. Depending on
whether your Bible breaks out and labels the various speeches
or notes the changes in voice with footnotes, it could be
considerably more difficult to follow than the normal psalm.

Where the *Song of Songs* really departs from the other
psalms is in its subject matter. This book is about human
romantic love. Here, for example, is the groom wooing
his bride:

> How beautiful you are, my darling!
> Oh, how beautiful!
> Your eyes behind your veil are doves.
> Your hair is like a flock of goats
>   descending from Mount Gilead.
>
>   Song of Songs 4:1

Granted, a modern bride might not appreciate the sentiment-
ality and lack of sophistication involved in having her hair
compared to a flock of mountain goats. But brides in those days
apparently swooned at that kind of talk. Though expressions
and manners of speech are always changing, human emotions
– such as love between a man and a woman – never do. And in
case you ever thought God was prudish about sex, reading this
book will be an enlightening experience. It shouldn't surprise
us, however, that the Creator has some understanding of the
physical and emotional dynamics which make romance and
marriage work.

In Retrospect

Five books of Moses, followed by twelve more books of
history, and now these five books of poetry or wisdom together
reveal the great diversity and depth of the anthology that is the
Bible. And we still have forty-four Bible books we've not yet
covered.

Job, Psalms, Proverbs, Ecclesiastes and the *Song of Songs* enhance the Bible's historical record, both in terms of breadth and depth. They broaden the Bible's selection of literature, and they deepen readers' understanding of the literature already there. Moreover, there are far more entry points for new Bible readers in this section of books than in either of the two sections that preceded it. No wonder the Bible's wisdom literature enjoys a readership equal to or greater than any of the Bible's other books. Fortunately, we've not seen all there is of biblical poetry. For the next section of books – the last section of Old Testament books – often employs poetry in the expression of prophecy.

7

The Books of Prophecy

With the books of Moses likened to Africa and the books of history to Asia, the books of prophecy can be compared to Europe. You'll recall that we paralleled the books of poetry to Australia. As Europe is slightly larger than Australia, so the books of prophecy take up slightly more room in the Bible than the books of poetry. Further, as Europe has a more direct connection with Asia than does Australia, so the books of prophecy have a more direct connection with the books of history than do the books of poetry.

There are seventeen books of prophecy. They begin with *Isaiah* and end with *Malachi*, closing the Old Testament section of the Bible. Like the books of poetry, they don't extend the time line of Israel's history; rather, they fill in the one laid down by the books of history. Apart from *Job*, most of the books of poetry were associated with the kings of Israel's glory days: David and Solomon. By contrast, the books of prophecy were associated mainly with the period of Israel's decline and fall.

The books of prophecy exhibit yet another distinct form of writing in the Bible. In order to appreciate these books, we need to clarify the meaning of prophecy. It's not what you might think.

The Nature of Biblical Prophecy

Many people today think of prophecy as foretelling the future. Either someone in the past has foretold (prophesied) something that is to happen in the present, or someone in the present is foretelling (prophesying) something that is to happen in the future. In other words, a prophet is one who predicts the future. While there is an element of this in the Bible's idea of prophecy, it's not the central thrust.

The Bible's idea of prophecy is a statement made on behalf of God, and a prophet is one who makes that statement. When God speaks, there *is* often an element of foretelling involved. Thus, when Moses warned Israel that they would enjoy the promised land if they obeyed the law and lose it if they disobeyed, he was acting in the role of prophet. When the prophet spoke, therefore, the future was fluid, depending on the listener's response to what God was saying. Contrast this with fortune-telling and crystal-ball-gazing which imply that the future is static and can be described as if it is just waiting to happen, regardless of what we do.

There were certain elements of Hebrew prophecy which spoke of the future in terms that human behaviour could not change. For example, a recurring promise of God was that He would one day defeat all Israel's enemies and usher in a period of great prosperity through a descendant of David. This descendant came to have many titles, the most memorable of which was 'Messiah'. The prophets affirmed this promise over and over, even when Israel's behaviour was at its worst.

But most prophecy, either implicitly or explicitly, offered a varying future, depending upon the hearers' response to the prophecy. One of the prophets, Jeremiah, put it this way (taken from Jeremiah 18):

This is the word that came to Jeremiah from the LORD: "Go down to the potter's house, and there I will give you my message." So I went down to the potter's house, and I saw him working at the wheel. But the pot he was shaping from the clay was marred in his hands; so the potter formed it into another pot, shaping it as it seemed best to him.

Then the word of the LORD came to me: "O house of Israel, can I not do with you as this potter does?" declares the LORD. "Like clay in the hand of the potter so are you in my hand, O house of Israel. If at any time

I announce that a nation or kingdom is to be uprooted, torn down and destroyed, and if that nation I warned repents of its evil, then I will relent and not inflict on it the disaster I had planned. And if at another time I announce that a nation or kingdom is to be built up and planted, and if it does evil in my sight and does not obey me, then I will reconsider the good I had intended to do for it.

"Now therefore say to the people of Judah and those living in Jerusalem, 'This is what the LORD says: Look! I am preparing a disaster for you and devising a plan against you. So turn from your evil ways, each one of you, and reform your ways and your actions.'"

As you can see, the thrust of God's prophecies are to encourage good human behaviour. Human behaviour – not forces beyond human control – determines whether the future will be bright or dismal.

Biblical prophecy is therefore more *moralistic* than *futuristic*. It emphasises the kind of living that secures a happy future and warns against behaviour that clouds that future. For this reason, the books of prophecy contain strong denunciations of evil with accompanying warnings of doom. What 'gloom and doom' these books possess, however, is more than offset by the expressions of hope that accompany their encouragement to good behaviour. Moreover, the background theme of God's continual good behaviour guarantees ultimate deliverance, since His behaviour has even more consequences than any human's. Thus, these books put forth rays of hope, even when they discuss the most discouraging of circumstances.

Nevertheless, there is no denying that the books of prophecy are largely words of warning. These prophecies arose in the context of the declining fortunes of Israel's kingdom. They have, therefore, a sense of immediacy. Calls for a moral lifestyle are given with a greater urgency than those found in the books of poetry. For this reason, these books are not as easy to read.

The Line of Prophets

Moses said that God would raise up prophets like him in the generations to follow. And so God did. The prophets did not possess administrative power like the kings. They didn't have a place in the tabernacle or temple rituals as did the priests. They simply spoke the mind of God as it was given to them.

They came from every walk of life, some quite humble. David was a king who was also a prophet. Jeremiah was a priest who was also a prophet. Amos was a sheepherder who was also a prophet.

Many of the prophets who followed Moses kept a relatively low profile. They might have delivered a message to a king or a city, but they did not fully occupy the people's attention as had Moses. Two possible exceptions were Elijah and Elisha who became very prominent in the days of the northern kingdom. A lot of their fame came from the miracles that God performed through them. Each of them, for instance, raised a dead child back to life. Not all the prophets exhibited miraculous powers. And even when they did, such powers were considered secondary to their main ministry of delivering God's message to their fellow citizens.

Some of the prophets' messages have been put into writing. Thus, we have seventeen books of prophecy. We don't have books from every prophet. We have no book of Elijah or Elisha, for example. Nor do we assume that the seventeen books we have comprise more than a portion of all that the prophets spoke in their various ministries. We can consider these books a sampling of all that the prophets spoke.

Unlike the kingship and the priesthood, the position of prophet could not be passed on to one's descendants. God chose in each generation those whom He would have to speak for Him. Each prophet stood firm in the revelation that had come through Moses and other prophets, and brought new light to that revelation. Although there were false prophets, none of them ever managed to get their words included in the Scriptures. The true prophets whose words were preserved saw their messages merely as a part of God's overall message.

The line of succession was God's doing, and the total message was His to convey. Each prophet was carrying a torch in a relay race.

Poetry in the Books of Prophecy

The prophets often gave their prophecies in the form of poetry. Here, for example, are the opening words of the first book of prophecy, *Isaiah*:

> Hear, O heavens! Listen, O earth!
>   For the LORD has spoken:
> "I reared children and brought them up,
>   but they have rebelled against me.
> The ox knows his master,
>   the donkey his owner's manger,
> but Israel does not know,
>   my people do not understand."

Isaiah 1:2–3

See the parallelism? Heavens, earth; reared, brought up; ox and master, donkey and owner's manger; knows, does not know; not know, not understand. See the picturesqueness? Farm animals. Remember that these are the marks of Hebrew poetry, and you will see them throughout the books of prophecy.

See also the emphasis on morality and present behaviour? God says His people have revolted against Him. And see that Isaiah is passing on God's message to the people? These are the marks of Hebrew prophecy, and you will see them over and over in these books, too.

Though you will find prose passages in these books, poetry is the vehicle to which the prophets constantly return. Why would the prophets choose poetry to express their messages? Several reasons.

First, poetry, even when it doesn't rhyme, makes for far more memorable speech than prose. Since the prophets' contemporaries generally *heard* the messages rather than *read* them, a message they could easily remember suited the purpose better than one they could hear but easily forget.

Second, the striking images of poetry go straight to the heart of a matter in a way that makes prose seem roundabout. For example, consider the irony of Isaiah's picture: farm animals, dumb by nature, have more than enough sense not to rebel against owners who supply food and shelter. Such imagery better captured the hearers' attention in the first place.

Third, poetry is heightened speech; it conveys maximum meaning and passion in the fewest possible words. In short it is eloquent. Given the issues that the prophets dealt with – life and death, glory and shame, hope and despair – you would not be surprised to find them using the most cloquent form of speech available to them.

Fitting the Prophets into History

Often the prophets dated themselves according to the reign of a particular king in Israel's history. Here, for example, is how Isaiah prefaced his book:

> The vision concerning Judah and Jerusalem that Isaiah
> son of Amoz saw during the reigns of Uzziah, Jotham,
> Ahaz and Hezekiah, kings of Judah.
>
> Isaiah 1:1

As you can see, Isaiah's ministry was spread over the reigns of four of Judah's kings. In various places in his book he made reference to which king was currently reigning. In this way, the work is given an historical context. And in this way the books of history and the books of prophecy dovetail. The books of history mention some of the prophets by name – Isaiah and Jeremiah, for instance. This, too, helps solidify the connection between the two sections of books.

However, not all the prophets frame all their words so clearly. It won't always be easy to relate each book of prophecy, or each portion thereof, to a specific historical period described in the books of history. The connections, even when they're there, aren't always uniform in structure or precise in content. In other words, not all the prophets prefaced their words following the structure Isaiah used at the beginning of his books. And even when they did, such a dating scheme doesn't narrow down events very precisely. It's like a journalist saying that something happened during his assignment at Westminster while Harold Wilson, James Callaghan, Margaret Thaicher and John Major were prime ministers. Therefore, most of the time you only have a general context. But most of the time, that's enough to get the gist of the prophet's message.

One last thing. An individual book of prophecy sometimes reads less like a unit and more like a string of units. These units are basically components of poetry, but can include prose sections, too. The chapter divisions are often a red herring for formulating the text into digestible thought. As you read through, some passages will speak clearly and forcefully. Others, you'll just feel like you're enduring. Only by surveying for yourself a whole book, or section of a book, will you know which are the good parts and which are the dull ones.

The Major Prophets

The first five books of prophecy are called the major prophets; the last twelve are called the minor prophets. The major-minor distinction is a reference not to the stature of the individual prophets, but to the size of the books themselves. *Isaiah*, for example, is longer than all twelve of the minor prophets put together.

The major prophets, however, are not uniformly long. *Isaiah, Jeremiah* and *Ezekiel* are all quite long. *Lamentations*, on the other hand, is as short as some of the minor prophets. But because its full title is *The Lamentations of Jeremiah*, it is placed immediately after the book of *Jeremiah* and thus included in the major prophets. The book of *Daniel*, while not as long as *Isaiah, Jeremiah* and *Ezekiel*, is still longer than any of the minor prophets.

Generally speaking, the major prophets are placed in historical order. Isaiah prophesied a century or so before the fall of the kingdom. Jeremiah prophesied right through the fall and wrote *Lamentations* as a witness to the destruction of Jerusalem. Ezekiel and Daniel were exiles of Jerusalem and wrote their books on the foreign soil of Babylon.

Isaiah

I've already shown you how Isaiah begins. He goes on to compare his beloved Jerusalem as having become as Sodom of old (see page 70 or Genesis 18 and 19). These are strong words. They indicated the extent to which morality in ancient Israel had declined in Isaiah's day. The message was not one of condemnation, but warning. Isaiah, and all the prophets, continually offered hope along these lines:

> ". . . If you are willing and obedient,
>   you will eat the best from the land;
> but if you resist and rebel,
>   you will be devoured by the sword."
>   For the mouth of the LORD
>   has spoken.
>   Isaiah 1:19–20

The people often recognised the echoes of Moses' warnings in the prophets' messages. This was the same warning Moses had given before the promised land was taken: your behaviour determines the level of prosperity you enjoy on the land. Thus, every prophet reinforced all the messages that had come before him. There were recurring themes in their various messages.

There were times when the people fully realised the seriousness of their moral failures. At those times, the prophets would wax eloquent about the glorious plans God had prepared for some indeterminant future time. You'll run across many such passages in *Isaiah*, especially in the last half of the book.

Isaiah has several prose sections which are identical to passages found in *Samuel-Kings*. There are various theories to explain this, but the undeniable result is that the message of *Isaiah* is rooted thoroughly in the history of Israel's kingdom.

The books of the New Testament frequently quote the books of the Old. Among the books of prophecy, *Isaiah* is quoted more often than any other. The lines of its poetry are particularly memorable and its themes especially grand. Though it's a long book, it's filled with thought-provoking images and emotion-laden scenes.

Jeremiah

The only two books in the Bible longer than *Isaiah* are *Psalms* and *Jeremiah*. Since *Psalms* is comprised of 150 distinct pieces, that makes *Jeremiah* the single book that will take you the longest sitting to complete. This book is not only longer than *Isaiah*, it's more difficult to read. While *Isaiah* has a few prose sections, *Jeremiah* has many. And *Jeremiah's* prose consists largely of narratives which describe the fall of Jerusalem at the hands of Babylon. While Isaiah prophesied that Israel would have to face destruction, Jeremiah had to live through that destruction. It was not a happy time.

Because of the times in which he lived, and the resulting tone of his message, Jeremiah is called 'the weeping prophet'. His writing does carry that same glorious long-term hope that is found in *Isaiah* and the rest of the prophets. However, the difficulties of the moment could not be ignored.

Each of the prophetic books adds to the historical record in some measure. They include details which confirm or give more material to that found in the books of history. While some prophetic books offer a small amount of new information, *Jeremiah* adds much. The middle of the book is taken up with descriptions of the various incidents that happened in the last days of the kingdom. As with *Isaiah, Jeremiah* has several sections where prophecies are spoken about Israel's neighbours. Babylon, for example, while it would defeat Israel, would one day have a day of reckoning for its own behaviour. Indeed, by New Testament times, Babylon was a fallen empire.

Lamentations

As I mentioned earlier, *Lamentations* is the work of Jeremiah. Before trying to read something so massive as the work titled with his name, you might want to try this one as a sample. *Lamentations* is a straightforward poem – no prose sections. It extends for only five chapters, so it is quite short. It compares in length and style with *Song of Songs*. *Lamentations* is slightly shorter and more direct (only a single speaker instead of bride, groom, and chorus). The biggest difference is subject matter. While *Song of Songs* deals with romantic love, *Lamentations* deals with the shame of the demise of a nation and, particularly, its capital city.

Jerusalem with its temple and surrounding culture was the pride of Israel. When Israel was at its height, foreign dignitaries came to admire and praise the city. Years of decline, slowed by occasional bursts of renewal, had long been warning of a fall to come. With the burning of Jerusalem came the weighty realisation that what all the prophets, beginning with Moses, had warned about had finally come to pass. Yet even in this sobering poem, one finds threads of hope for the future.

Like *Ruth, Esther* and *Song of Songs*, the book of *Lamentations* offers you a chance to sample a significant portion of the Bible without biting off more than you can chew. If you can find fifteen or twenty uninterrupted minutes, and you're in a mood to handle a sombre poem, then this work will give you clear insight into the mind of a prophet. One of the things you'll see is that the prophets cared intensely for their fellow Israelites. While the destruction was a result of the nation's immorality and unwillingness to heed the prophets' warnings, the prophets' compassion was not stifled. It's a wonderful love to see.

Ezekiel

Ezekiel is one of the hardest books to read in the Bible. It's long. Its tone is sombre like *Jeremiah's*. And its images are more complex and harder to understand. You can enjoy reading this book, but that interest probably won't come until you've digested and absorbed some of the Bible's easier portions. Babylon besieged Israel for a number of years before the capital, Jerusalem, finally fell. During those years of siege, captives were taken from the land and shipped to Babylon. Ezekiel was one of those captives. He wrote his words while living in exile. If you thought exile from the promised land was the end of Israel's story, Ezekiel quickly convinces you otherwise.

First, he dealt at length with the problems that caused Israel to lose her land. He addressed them because behaviour remains a factor in the destiny of nations and individuals. As a prophet, Ezekiel was not about to let his fellow citizens forget that. He wanted them to learn from their mistakes and reform their lives, even though they were living on foreign soil. God could still look after His people there. Hadn't He taken care of them in the desert before they ever entered the promised land?

Second, Ezekiel wanted his people to maintain hope for the future. Toward that end he offered, in the last nine chapters, a vision of a glorious temple that would one day replace the one that Solomon built and Nebuchadnezzar of Babylon destroyed. Ezekiel gave no timetable for this glorious future, but all those images of future glory were being accumulated in people's minds. This hope carried them through the hardships they faced as they lived in subjection before their captors.

Daniel

Like *Ezekiel, Daniel* has some complicated images which are hard to understand and digest easily. These images add further to the glorious picture of the future of Israel. The central figure in that future was Messiah. Therefore, the image of hope could be triggered with the mention of just that word.

The complex imagery of *Daniel* shows up in the second half of the book. The first half, by contrast, is straightforward narrative. In fact, the stories in this section are some of the Bible's most beloved. They include Shadrach, Meshach, and Abednego in the fiery furnace, Daniel in the lion's den, and the story that gave rise to the proverbial saying, 'You could see the handwriting on the 'wall'.

Like the man Ezekiel, the man Daniel was an exiled Israelite. Daniel was assigned to service in King Nebuchadnezzar's court. He and his compatriots found themselves in several rather sticky situations. The Israelites had been taught to worship but one God. All the surrounding cultures, including Babylon, subscribed to polytheism. Each nation had its own god or gods. And often the king himself was deified. Since Daniel and his friends were determined to stay monotheistic, clashes with superiors were inevitable. The stories of how God delivered His people are fascinating and reminiscent of other great stories in earlier books of the Bible.

The Minor Prophets

The last twelve books in the Bible are quite short. Together, they're not quite as long as *Isaiah* by itself. In some Jewish Bibles they're combined and titled as one book. Though their messages are brief, they are still important. And each individual prophet has something special to contribute to the whole.

As the major prophets are organised in historical order, so also are the minor prophets. This doesn't mean, however, that the minor prophets followed the major prophets. They coexisted with them. Hosea, for example, was a contemporary of Isaiah. Therefore, just as the sequence of major prophets could be overlaid on the historical time frame sketched out by the books of history, so the sequence of minor prophets can be overlaid in the same time frame. In other words, the minor prophets also prophesied near the end of the kingdom.

Since the fall of Jerusalem is dated by historians at 586 BC, all the books of prophecy – major and minor – can be dated within a century or two of that date. The earlier prophets such as Isaiah (major) and Hosea (minor) would be dated a century or two before that date. The prophets of the exile, such as Ezekiel (major) and Daniel (major), would fall right around that date. And the prophets associated with the return to Israel after the exile, such as Haggai (minor),

Zechariah (minor), and Malachi (minor), would be dated within a century or two after that date. While all of the major prophets were associated with the Southern Kingdom, some of the minor prophets were connected with the Northern Kingdom, which fell in 722 BC. The fall for them would, therefore, be about a century and a half earlier than that of the Southern Kingdom.

If you're interested in dates that are more specific than this, Bible scholars are quick to supply them. The scholars don't always agree though. And they have been known to change their estimates with new archaeological finds. Such details are only likely to complicate your reading of these books at this point, not enhance it.

The relative shortness of these books makes them tempting to read. But like the major prophets, they are messages spoken in the context of the fall of the kingdom of Israel. Making the connections with that setting requires an understanding of the history that comes from other books. (This isn't true, for example, of Psalm 23 which can be read independently of any specific historical context.) For this reason, just keep in mind the general tenor of the prophets' times and the general thrust of their messages while reading any individual book. Don't worry about making detailed connections with specific historical circumstances. In other words, don't expect the book to be as easy to follow as Psalm 1 or Psalm 23, and you will still be able to get some meaning out of it.

Hosea

Hosea uses the figure of marriage to portray the relationship of God with Israel. He portrays God as a faithful and forgiving husband and Israel as an adulterous wife. If fact, he applies the word 'harlot' to Israel. Hosea's own experiences with a wayward wife are used to illustrate God's pain in dealing with Israel. The sins of Israel are spelled out. The exhortation is for Israel to 'Return to the LORD your God'.

Joel

The theme of *Joel* is the day of the Lord. This 'day of the Lord' shows up in other prophetic books, too. The day of the Lord is a day of reckoning, a day of judgment. It refers to a time when God brings down the wicked and haughty and lifts up the humble. Israel's exodus from Egypt was a type of day of the Lord. The Egyptian slavemasters were brought down, and humble Israelite slaves were raised to nationhood. Therefore, the day of the Lord meant destruction for some and deliverance for others. Joel spoke of a day of the Lord on the horizon for Israel. It was not exempt from God's judgments.

Amos

Amos prophesied about the same time as Hosea and Joel. He was a sheepherder who left his flocks to denounce the sins of his people, and especially those of the leaders. Moses' law demanded even more of the leaders than of the rank and file Israelites. Kings were to bring justice to the land. Power was a trust for which a king was held accountable. Like the other prophets, Amos was unafraid to confront the powerful.

Obadiah

Obadiah is the shortest book in the Old Testament – one chapter long. Like Joel, he emphasised the coming day of the Lord. He said that since all nations have a day of reckoning, it does not pay to gloat when another nation encounters misfortune. He also emphasised the principle, 'As you have done, it will be done to you'.

Jonah

Jonah marks a distinct change of pace. There is narrative here. Jonah tells his own story about how he first avoided delivering a message of warning to the great city of Nineveh, capital of Assyria. Israel's prophets often had words for surrounding nations, and Jonah was reluctant to deliver a message of repentance to this enemy of his people. His humbling experience with a great fish succeeded in turning him around. Nineveh responded positively to his message. Everyone, from the king on down, admitted that they had been living immorally. In the end, Jonah got a lesson in the depth of God's mercy.

Micah

With *Micah* we return to the normal poetic style of the prophets. There is a passage here that is identical to one in *Isaiah* about what will happen in 'the last days'. This phrase alluded to the coming time of Messiah. Micah reminded the people of all that God had done for them in the past. He called them to obedience in the present and hopefulness for the future. He spoke to both the people of the Northern Kingdom and those of the Southern Kingdom.

Nahum

Like Jonah, Nahum was concerned with the city of Nineveh. Only in *Nahum*, there is no narrative to accompany the prophecy. In *Jonah*, we were only given the gist of his message – a line or two. In *Nahum* we have God's full indictment of the city's wrong-doing. Nahum lived well after Jonah. Nineveh's embrace of morality had ended, and Nahum found himself warning of their final fall. Historians record that this demise occurred in 612 BC.

Habakkuk

Habakkuk foresaw the assault on Israel by Babylon and asked a question worthy of Job. That is, he admitted Israel's sin but asked why an unrighteous nation like Babylon was so worthy to conquer. There is no lengthy answer in this short book. God's pithy response is that the righteous person lives by faith. That is, he or she trusts that all accounts are eventually settled. If a nation like Babylon overcomes today, they will surely have their own day of reckoning tomorrow. Therefore, once again the people were exhorted to live righteously.

Zephaniah

With Zephaniah we come to a contemporary of Jeremiah. Zephaniah's prophecy came in the years immediately preceding the fall of Jerusalem. Zephaniah talked about the coming day of the Lord, which for Jerusalem was right around the corner. Yet he, too, spoke of the glorious long-term future God had in mind for His people.

Haggai

The remaining three minor prophets did their work after the remnant of Israelites had returned from exile in Babylon. Haggai is specifically mentioned in the book of *Ezra* as being among the returning exiles. He encouraged the governor and high priest who were in office in those days. Specifically, he encouraged the leaders and the people not to grieve over the diminished stature of the nation they were rebuilding, for God was going to do something even greater down the road.

This is, once again, the great long-term hope that the prophets were continually bringing. The particular significance here is that the rebuilding of Jerusalem did not constitute that great hope. That gave some idea of how great the future glory was to be: it wouldn't just be a repeat of the past glory, but something that would be far greater.

Zechariah

Zechariah was a contemporary and co-worker of Haggai's. He, too, is mentioned in the book of *Ezra*. His writing is considerably longer and more complex than Haggai's. He described visions that are reminiscent of some of the complex imagery found in *Ezekiel* and the second half of *Daniel*. There are lines and passages that inspire, but the book as a whole can bewilder you rather easily.

Malachi

The twelfth and last of the minor prophets is Malachi. His prophecy is more prose-like than poetic. He was concerned with the moral stature of the priesthood in his time. You would think that after all the warning the prophets had given before the fall of Jerusalem, and all the chastening Israel had experienced with the fall, that the priests of the nation would be ever diligent about their duties. Not so. Malachi warned that while Israel's great future still lay ahead, it would not be a great day for those who took the Lord's morals lightly. Priests who thought they would get a 'free ride' would find a rude surprise.

Thus, the last Old Testament prophet sounded the same note as Moses had at the beginning: not to think that their victory over the Canaanites guaranteed them a 'free ride' in the promised land. Behaviour matters. Even when you're the chosen people of God.

The Completion of the Old Testament Books

We have now covered the books of Moses, of history, of poetry and of prophecy. Together these comprise what has come to be called the Old Testament. The books of Moses and history are arranged in chronological order. Together they outline the historical period of the entire Old Testament. The books of poetry are in a chronological order which can be superimposed on the Old Testament time frame. Also to be superimposed on this basic order are the major prophets, and, finally, the minor prophets.

Overlaying these chronological orders gives the proper historical perspective on these thirty-nine books. Without this perception, you might think they were written or occurred one after the other If you tried to read them all in sequence, you might become tangled in confusion. Now that you recognise distinct sections of books and know some facts about each individual book, you can better decide where you want to start and how you want to proceed.

But before you start reading too much, let me tell you about the rest of the Bible. There's only a fourth of it left to cover. But that fourth is a completion and fulfilment of all that we've read so far. Besides, some of its books are also easy to read. Let's finish this last leg of our book-by-book journey.

8

The Four Gospels

Leaving the continents of the eastern hemisphere, we now
turn to those of the western hemisphere. That is, as we saw
distinct sections of books in the Old Testament, so we will
find distinct sections in the New. We can liken the Gospels to
North America, *Acts* to the narrow isthmus of Central America,
and the epistles to South America.

Dividing the Bible into Old Testament and New has some
usefulness, just as being able to separate the world into Old
World and New. But recognising the distinct sections of books
within the Bible is even more useful, just as being able to
recognise all the particular continents is more useful.

New Testament Times

The main difference between the New Testament and the Old is
time. The last events recorded in the Old Testament were those
associated with the return from exile. That means at least three
or four centuries elapsed between that return and the time of
Jesus of Nazareth. This 'silent' period between the testaments
is comparable in length to the time that the judges ruled and
also to the time that the kings ruled. It's also about the same
number of years between when Joseph went to Egypt and when
Moses led the Israelite descendants out.

The expressions 'Old Testament' and 'New Testament'
originated with the prophet Jeremiah. When he was talking
about the glorious future for Israel that the prophets often spoke
of, he said that God would 'make a new covenant with the
house of Israel' (Jeremiah 31). 'Testament' was synonymous

with 'covenant', and thus 'new testament' alludes to Jeremiah's promise. What unifies the New Testament books to each other and to the Scriptures written previously is the conviction that Jesus of Nazareth was the long-promised Messiah. Thus, upon Jesus were fixed all the hopes of a glorious future that had been promised over and over by Jeremiah and all the prophets.

The books of the New Testament were, therefore, not written to be a departure from the Old Testament books. Quite to the contrary, they were written as a fulfilment. In the same way, *Exodus* (occurring some three or four centuries after the events that closed the book of *Genesis*) was not presented as a departure from the promises God made to Abraham, Isaac and Jacob in the book of *Genesis*, but rather a fulfilment of them. Likewise, the New Testament books present themselves as the fulfilment of the promises made throughout the Old Testament books.

The terms 'Old Testament' and 'New Testament' originated from Jeremiah's prophecy but didn't come into use until after all sixty-six books were gathered. Only then did the occasion present itself to separate the writings into two separate sections. In other words, the New Testament books speak only of the Scriptures – never of 'this testament' or 'that'.

The Messianic Prophecies

You could probably tell from my description of all the Bible books to this point that there is no single book, or even passage, you could refer to which would tell you everything you wanted to know about the Messiah. The references to this figure are scattered throughout the books: a line here, a few lines there. In fact, the term 'messiah' only occurs two times in the entire Old Testament. But this future personality was referred to in a number of ways, and 'Messiah' was only one of them.

The term 'Son of David' was generally considered a Messianic title. Other titles used include 'the Coming One', 'the Righteous One' and 'the Son of God'. Any reference to a figure of great stature who would one day lead Israel to its greatest glory was considered a reference to the Messiah.

Many of the prophetic references focused either additionally or exclusively on the glorious kingdom that Messiah would rule. Some references which mentioned 'the last days', 'the coming kingdom', or even 'the day of the Lord', were a reminder of pending judgment. In other places, these phrases were understood to be referring to Messiah's time, even though He Himself may not have been mentioned in the same breath. The context tells which future event the audience was intended to recognise.

Not only were references to Messiah and His kingdom scattered throughout the Scriptures, many of those references were obscure. It was not immediately clear exactly what the prophecy was driving at, what kind of portrait it was painting.

Taking the sun total of the prophecies about the Messianic times, no one knew quite what to expect. The prophecies included descriptions of pain, suffering, and humiliation. They also included descriptions of power, exaltation, and glory. How do you reconcile such conflicting images? The position of the New Testament writers was that Jesus fulfilled the fuzzy picture and made it all clear. For example, pain, suffering, and humiliation could be seen in His crucifixion, while power, exaltation and glory could be seen in His resurrection.

Jesus was not proclaimed to be the Messiah until after His resurrection and ascension into heaven. Until then, His messianic identity was kept under wraps. During His earthly ministry, Jesus would use an oblique messianic reference to Himself – such as 'the son of man', a term found mostly in the obscure book of *Ezekiel*. Once Jesus was raised from the dead, His disciples could recognise what He was driving at, but until that time His messianic identity was not a major item. This explains why, though the Gospels present Jesus as the Messiah, they also present Him as seeming to sidestep the issue.

Not everyone believes that Jesus is the Messiah or that, as such, He fulfills all the prophecies associated with messianic times. But this is the position of all those who wrote the books in the New Testament. As the Gospels record His life, it was remarkable enough to capture attention, even if it had not been a fulfilment of prophecy. But that His life was a fulfilment of what the Scriptures had long promised is stressed again and again.

With Jesus, 'the last days' have come; the glorious future promised by the prophets is 'at hand'. The 'seed of David' has taken His throne, and that throne is one even more glorious than anyone had anticipated: heaven itself. Jesus' resurrection from the dead and ascension into heaven inaugurated the fulfilling of all that the Old Testament books had promised. Thus, the New Testament is utterly dependent upon the Old Testament for its greatest meaning.

What Is a Gospel?

The term 'gospel' means 'good news' or 'glad tidings'. In each of the four Gospels, Jesus is presented as the 'good news' or 'glad tidings' of ultimate redemption that the prophets had so often heralded. The titles *Matthew, Mark, Luke* and *John* are short for *The Gospel According to Matthew*, and so on. Even this is a short form for *The Gospel of Jesus Christ According to Matthew*, and so on. 'Christ' is the Greek term for the Hebrew term 'Messiah'. Every reference to Jesus as 'Jesus Christ' or, more simply, 'the Christ', is a reference to His being the Messiah.

Since each of the Gospels is about Jesus, you could think of them as biographies. But their forms and styles are very different from most biographies. For one thing, we are told very little about Jesus's life before He entered public ministry at about the age of thirty. There is mention of the circumstances of His birth and of an incident that occurred when He was twelve years old. Biographies normally include this kind of background.

There are two fundamental reasons why the Gospels focus almost entirely on the years of Jesus's public ministry. First, the Gospels were written as eyewitness accounts. The eyewitnesses were the followers He attracted during His ministry. The events of the ministry were the events to which they could attest: 'This is what we saw and heard.' Second, the promises that the prophets had made about the Messiah had to do, not so much with his childhood and early adulthood, but with what He would do in His maturity. Thus, the emphasis in the Gospels was on His ministry as opposed to His formative years.

Some Bibles will read, for example, *The Gospel According to Saint Matthew*. 'Saint' means 'holy one' and is a sign of respect to those who wrote the Gospels. It is also applied to others who wrote New Testament books, so that we have *Saint* Peter and *Saint* Paul. But as you read the New Testament books, you'll see that 'saint' was a term generally applied to all those who believed in Jesus at that time. Recognising this, many of the modern translations simply leave off the 'Saint'.

The Gospels follow closely in the tradition of the books of history we saw in the Old Testament. Only in this case, instead of the subject being a line of judges or line of kings, the subject is a single individual. The description, as with the books of history, is of words spoken and deeds done. Little is told of the inward thoughts and motivations of the various characters. The authors of the books make few if any references to themselves. Therefore, the same reading strategy that works for the books of history will work for the four Gospels.

The General Storyline of the Gospels.

The Gospels tell how Jesus was born as a descendant of David. To be descended from David was an essential requirement of the Messiah, according to the prophecies in the Scripture. Genealogies are included to support the claim. He was described as being born in Bethlehem, having sojourned for a time in Egypt, and having been raised in Galilee. Again, the prophets had made reference to all three places in their descriptions of the Messiah, so the mention of such details was important to the Gospel writers.

When He was about thirty years old, Jesus was baptised in the Jordan River by John the Baptist. John was another in the long line of Israel's prophets. He preached that the nation should repent of its sins and offered the experience of being baptised to symbolise the cleansing that came with the forgiveness of sins. John knew that Jesus was a prophet even greater than he was. When Jesus came to be baptised along with everyone else, John said their roles should be reversed. Jesus insisted that John baptise Him, and so it was.

Jesus then went to the wilderness where He spent forty days fasting and being tempted by the devil. At the end of that time, He began His own ministry. It mirrored John's in some ways. Both preached repentance for the forgiveness of sins. Both proclaimed that God's long promised kingdom was at hand. But Jesus's ministry was attended with miracle after miracle; John's ministry was far more tame.

Jesus's miracles included giving sight to the blind, giving hearing to the deaf, healing crippled people so they could walk, and even raising the dead on several occasions. So many were the miracles that one of the Gospel writers said that, if they were all written down, not even the world could contain the books. Hyperbole, perhaps. But it conveys that the miracles were more commonplace than occasional.

Not all the miracles had to do with healing disease and death. Jesus also multiplied some fish and a few loaves of bread into a feast for thousands. He walked on water, too. All these miracles were performed to meet pressing human need. The closest He came to a feat for show was when He commanded a fig tree to wither, and that was to give an object lesson to His disciples. In fact, when asked to perform some spectacular feat to prove that He was not a false prophet, He refused. He wanted to be judged strictly by the acts of compassion He had been showing to the citizens of Israel.

Jesus spent His ministry travelling around the country, teaching about God and visiting the sick, hungry and discouraged. The miracles provided surges of power that can overshadow the simplicity of His lifestyle. He simply went from place to place, doing good for people. The miracles were a sign that God was involved in His good deeds.

Each Gospel is a collection of various episodes in Jesus's life, strung together in order. There are two other kinds of incidents recorded besides his teaching sessions and acts of kindness. The first sort were the challenges He received from the religious authorities of His day. The more popular His ministry became with the masses, the more charges the authorities levelled at him. The other kind of episodes recorded were His private teaching sessions to His closest disciples. It was in these more secluded times that He let his identity as Messiah become known.

Jesus's public ministry never made an issue of His being the Messiah. In fact, He did all He could to discourage such speculation when He encountered it. He ministered as a humble servant of God, the same way that all Israel's prophets before Him had ministered. His closest disciples guessed that He was more than just a prophet, that He was indeed the long awaited Messiah. He privately affirmed this to them, but warned them not to make it public until after He had been crucified and raised from the dead.

Jesus's disciples were slow to believe that He would be put to death. And they were not sure what rising from the dead might mean. But soon enough, the pressures against Jesus reached a boiling point. Israel was under Roman occupation at the time. Jewish and Roman authorities conspired to have Jesus crucified – nailed to a cross. For non-Romans this was the normal means of execution in those days when the death penalty was required. Roman citizens condemned to die received the less gruesome punishment of being beheaded.

Though Jesus had told His disciples that He would rise from the dead on the third day, they were all surprised to find the tomb empty when they went to check it. They had been thoroughly demoralised by His crucifixion. His resurrection stirred them; it lifted them from the depths and took them to the heights. On this note, each of the Gospels ends.

The Gospels emphasise the last week of Jesus's earthly life – the week that concluded with a crucifixion on Friday and a resurrection on Sunday. There is more written about this time than any other period in His ministry. It's understandable that the events of this week would make the most vivid impression on the disciples.

The Teaching of Jesus

While the Gospels themselves will remind you of the Bible's books of history, the teaching of Jesus will remind you of the Bible's books of poetry and prophecy. Consider, for example, the Beatitudes as an example of Hebrew poetry:

> "Blessed are the poor in spirit,
>   for theirs is the kingdom of heaven.
> Blessed are those who mourn,
>   for they will be comforted.
> Blessed are the meek,
>   for they will inherit the earth . . ."
>   Matthew 5:3–5

Note the parallelism built around the word 'blessed'. Even the word 'blessed' harkens back to the first psalm's, 'Blessed is the man . . .' The Lord's prayer bears the marks of having been born from a poetic Hebrew mindset:

> "'Our Father in heaven,
> hallowed be your name,
> Your kingdom come,
> your will be done
>   on earth as it is in heaven . . .'"
>   Matthew 6:9–10

Note the repetitions: 'your name', 'your kingdom', and 'your will'. Note the symmetry of beginning with 'in heaven' and coming full circle to end on the same note. Note the picturesque contrast of heaven above and earth below, and how the idea is to make the beauty of the heavens extend to the earth. God's name being hallowed, His Kingdom coming, and His will being done, successively and successfully express the extension of God's heavenly rule to the places where we live.

Jesus's teaching thus resembles, both in style and-substance, the teaching of the prophets long before Him. Presented in the setting of the history of His ministry, that teaching was highly moral in content and highly poetic in casing. Jesus also spoke of the future as the prophets did, although from His perspective that future was not dim and distant, but rather 'at hand'. Remembering this, you can view the Gospels as a hybrid of the writing styles you have seen so far in the Scriptures: history combined with poetry and prophecy.

Some of Jesus's statements, when taken out of context, seem hard to understand. He said, for example:

> "If anyone comes to me and does not hate his
> father and mother, his wife and children,
> his brothers and sisters, – yes, even his
> own life – he cannot be my disciple . . ."
>
> Luke 14:26

Hearing the words 'hate his . . .', some people take Jesus to be speaking of a literal hate. But this is a figure of speech, a Hebrew idiom for showing preference. He said in another place:

> "No-one can serve two masters. Either he
> will hate the one and love the other, or he
> will be devoted to the one and despise the
> other. You cannot serve both God and Money."
>
> Matthew 6:24

In this passage, the figure of speech is more obvious. He's not saying that a person with two masters feels radically opposing emotions towards them. He's saying that one master is going to get the better treatment. Some of Jesus's statements, which may seem strange when standing alone, will make much more sense as you read them in their historical and linguistic settings.

Jesus's individual statements are best understood in the context of all He taught. And all He taught is best understood before the backdrop of the Old Testament – from which He derived all His teaching.

The First Three Gospels

The first three Gospels are all fairly similar to each other. They follow the same general outline of events, though each offers a different perspective and different details about events. It's like reading eyewitness accounts of a road accident at a junction by three witnesses who each stood on three different corners of the junction.

Matthew

From among His followers, Jesus picked twelve to travel with Him and assist Him in His ministry. Matthew was one of these twelve. He also went by the name of Levi. He had formerly been a tax collector. This was a despised occupation in those days, particularly because the tax-gatherers were considered accomplices to the Roman occupation. Matthew's involvement typified how Jesus reached out even to the outcasts of that society.

Chapters five to seven of this Gospel give the Sermon on the Mount. This is the longest uninterrupted teaching of Jesus recorded in the Bible. It develops the theme Jesus constantly returned to throughout His ministry: the kingdom of God. Or, as Matthew usually referred to it, the kingdom of heaven. The terms are synonymous. Included in the Sermon on the Mount are the Beatitudes and the Lord's prayer.

Matthew quotes the Old Testament prophecies about the Messiah more than any other Gospel. And his is the only Gospel that begins with a genealogy. It seems clear that Matthew is anticipating Jewish readers who will be aware of the many prophecies, and thus need abundant explanation of how Jesus fulfils them.

Mark

Mark in many ways is like a miniature *Matthew*, being a third shorter. *Mark* is, in fact, the shortest Gospel of all. If you want a look at the life of Jesus, it would be the best Gospel with which to start.

Mark was a protégé of Peter's. For this reason, *Mark* is sometimes thought of as 'Peter's Gospel'. Though it is the shortest of the Gospels, it includes details and events that none of the other Gospels have. While *Matthew* emphasises Jesus's teaching, including His parables, *Mark* focuses on Jesus's action, the deeds.

Luke

Luke is the longest of the four Gospels. Though *Matthew* is divided into more chapters (twenty-eight compared to twenty-four), *Luke* actually has more text. For some reason, those who made the chapter divisions carved up fewer and longer chapters in *Luke*. Obviously, *Luke* contains a number of details absent in *Matthew* and *Mark*.

Luke was a protégé of the apostle Paul's. Luke himself didn't claim to be an eyewitness to the life of Jesus. Rather, he offered his work as a collection of eyewitness accounts that he had gathered and put in order. This helps explain why his account was particularly long and rich. Through Paul's travels and relationships, Luke had access to many of those who knew Jesus personally. This included His mother Mary who is the likely source for the extended narrative describing Jesus's birth.

Luke addresses his Gospel in the first few lines to someone named Theophilus. This name means 'one who loves God'. Whether the name refers to a specific individual, or is used as a metaphor for God-fearing people in general, is unclear from the text itself. What is clear is that Luke worked hard to research all the accounts which he included. He particularly took care to align the accounts in consecutive order. He wishes the reader to gain the benefit of the exact knowledge which he painstakingly assembled.

Luke contains a condensed version of the Sermon on the Mount, including condensed Beatitudes and Lord's prayer. Such condensations point out the 'idea' orientation of the

Gospels. That is, we are being given the gist of what Jesus taught as various people heard it and remembered it. He was not followed about by people taking this words down in shorthand, or by reporters preserving it all on tape recorders for later transcription. Thus, while the Gospel accounts may vary in details, they all convey the same messages about the kinds of things Jesus said and did. This 'idea' orientation is true of all the Scriptures. The exact words are important, but only because they are the means of conveying the ideas which are more important.

Luke is the only author of a Bible book who might be considered to be a non-Jew. This possibility stems from a reference Paul makes to Luke as a Gentile. If this is so, it helps explain why Luke gives less emphasis to Jesus's Jewish credentials than Matthew does. While not ignoring how Jesus fulfilled prophecy, Luke emphasises His humanity and compassion – qualities which would appeal to readers from any nation.

The Fourth Gospel

The last Gospel, *John*, is of a very different style from the first three. The story outline is the same: public ministry preceded by John the Baptist and concluded with crucifixion and resurrection. But the way that story is told is quite different.

John

While the other Gospels string together many specific episodes in the life of Jesus, *John* chooses to focus on a relative few. In doing so, the book gives each incident greater treatment. For example, the other Gospels tell the story of Jesus miraculously feeding the multitude in a few lines. *John* devotes a lengthy chapter to the incident.

John saw each event as revealing deep and profound things about Jesus and about God. The feeding of the multitudes spoke of humanity's need for spiritual, as well as physical, nourishment. The healing of a blind man shows our natural blindness to truth and our need to be healed. The healing of a crippled man displays our paralysis of fear and our need to be able to take steps of faith. With the description of each incident, John includes extensive remarks by Jesus. These discourses included interaction – both queries and challenges – from disciples and critics.

John devotes five chapters (John 13 to 17) to recording things Jesus said the night before He died. Through John's words we are able to get a more fully developed picture of Jesus's own thinking and the way He perceived His ministry and mission.

John was one of the twelve disciples, along with Matthew and Peter. He had been a fishing partner with Peter before Jesus began His ministry. John outlived most of the other twelve disciples. He wrote His Gospel in the twilight of His life. Since the other Gospels had clearly established the facts of Jesus's ministry, John was free to reflect more on the meaning behind those facts. His years of reflection, along with his willingness to embark upon a different style of narrative, adds to our understanding of Jesus in a significant way.

Now What?

The story of Jesus's earthly life, including His resurrection from the dead, has been told. This story has enormous implications for all of humanity. The rest of the Bible's books help us begin to explore those implications.

9

The Book of Acts

All that separates us from the remaining continent of South
America is the narrow isthmus that connects it with North
America. *Acts* is the book that links the Gospels with the
epistles. *Acts* is short for *The Acts of the Apostles*. As the
Gospels described the ministry of Jesus, *Acts* describes the
ministry of His apostles. For this reason we ought to clarify
what is meant by apostles.

Disciples and Apostles

Jesus's ministry attracted a great deal of attention. The Gospels
describe how 'multitudes' followed Him. No doubt many were
attracted by the miracles, and even by the crowds themselves.
But many were very interested in His teaching. Those who
sought that teaching were called disciples. 'Disciple' relates to
the word 'discipline' and refers to a person taking the position
of pupil, student, or learner, with Jesus as the instructor,
teacher, or rabbi. From among those disciples, Jesus chose
certain individuals to be apostles. 'Apostle' literally means
'sent one'. These select disciples were chosen and equipped
to be teachers of the message. Thus, all apostles are disciples,
but not all disciples are apostles.

Perhaps the best known apostles are the twelve that Jesus
chose to accompany Him as He travelled about ministering.
These included Peter and John, whom we've already discussed.
These two, along with John's brother James, constituted an
inner circle within the inner circle of the twelve. Jesus also
worked with larger groups of apostles, too. There was one

occasion, for example, when He sent out seventy to minister in His name: to preach and teach His message, while also performing the same works of kindness and power. Thus, there were numerous apostles. Whatever their numbers, however, they were always a subset of the much larger group known as disciples.

Another well-known apostle was named Paul. He isn't mentioned in the four Gospels because he was selected after Jesus had ascended into heaven. Even though he was a late arrival to the apostolic corps, he did not fail to make a significant contribution. He became one of the best known of all the apostles. *The Acts of the Apostles*, in fact, devotes more attention to his acts than to any of the other apostles.

The Luke-Acts Connection

Acts was written by Luke, the same one who wrote a Gospel. He begins *Acts* with a salutation to Theophilus and a reference to 'my former book' (the Gospel of *Luke*). We could, therefore, dub his two books 'The Acts of Jesus' and 'The Acts of the Apostles'. They comprise a two-volume history of New Testament times.

The events described in *Acts* took place over several decades. *Acts*, therefore, extends the time line of the historical record laid down by the Gospels. As the books of Moses and history established the historical framework for the rest of the Old Testament, so Gospels-*Acts* establish the historical framework for the rest of the New Testament. As the books of poetry and prophecy fitted in and filled in the Old Testament historical record, so the epistles fit in and fill in the New Testament historical record.

There is a symmetry in the *Luke-Acts* portrayal of history. They are about the same length. The first volume of this history portrays Jesus as ministering on earth; the second portrays Him as alive and ministering from heaven. The first reveals how Jesus fit the prophecies of a suffering Messiah; the second reveals how Jesus fit the prophecies of a reigning Messiah. The first describes how Jesus trained disciples; the second describes their full transformation into apostles, who themselves trained even more disciples. The first was a book about an individual helping others; the second was about many individuals helping many others. The first was localised in Israel and particularly Jerusalem; the second saw the message of Jesus spread around the world. Thus, the second volume proves the implicit thesis of the first: that trying to stop Jesus, even with the ultimate weapon of death, only made Him more effective.

Luke's Association with Paul

Luke doesn't give equal treatment to all the apostles in *Acts*. In fact, if you're looking for a 'Whatever Happened to the twelve Apostles', you'll be disappointed. Instead, Luke focuses on the activities of Peter, and even more so on the activities of Paul. Luke probably drew from the same sources that had provided him information for his Gospel. They would have also witnessed the events that occurred in Jerusalem the first few days, weeks and years after the resurrection. And as for many of the events involving Paul which occurred even later, Luke himself was an eyewitness.

Paul recruited many assistants to help him in his work as an apostle. Luke was one of those helpers. Paul makes fleeting references to Luke, as he does to many of his co-workers, in some of his letters. Luke is called 'the beloved physician', perhaps indicating his trade or former occupation. In the later parts of *Acts*, Luke's narrative occasionally shifts into first person plural, indicating those events for which Luke himself was a firsthand witness.

Luke's emphasis on Paul and Peter doesn't appear to be born of any desire to exalt these men above the other apostles. The explanation seems to be a practical one. That is, Luke's intent was to pass on eyewitness accounts, and so his writing was limited to those accounts that he could obtain.

Jesus had sent His apostles into the whole world with His message. Since these men were sent to every point on the compass, it's not surprising that many of them lost touch with each other over the years. Peter's activities were easier to trace.

First, he was looked up to as a leader, or even *the* leader, among the twelve. Second, in the early years he focused his work in and around Jerusalem. Paul and Luke would visit Jerusalem on their travels and, thereby, hear from Peter or those who had witnessed Peter's work. Of course, Luke's lengthy personal association with Paul gave him an abundance of material to include in the book.

The Fragmentary Nature of New Testament History

We may wish to know a lot more about the life of Jesus than the four Gospels tell us. Yet those accounts seem to describe abundantly the few years of Jesus's ministry when compared to *Acts*, which is all we have to tell us of the few decades that followed. But the little we have recorded of the history of New Testament times is more than anyone had in the years while the history was being made.

The apostles initially spread their message of Jesus's resurrection by travelling from town to town and speaking face-to-face with as many people as they could. They didn't sit down first to write the Gospels, much less the book of *Acts*. The writing came later, usually when they realised they were approaching the end of their lives and would no longer be around to bear witness to what they had seen and heard of the carpenter from Nazareth.

Spreading the message of Jesus was a dangerous occupation. The apostles faced persecution on every side. Premature death was almost a certainty for them. Often death was preceded by imprisonment. Prison provided the time, and impending death the reason, for them to commit their knowledge to writing. Such circumstances only allowed them to record what they deemed most important at the time.

Consequently, we aren't reading books that were written as an exhaustive history of the times by scholars applying years of research. Rather, we are reading documents produced in the face of death by men recording those things that were considered worth dying for. Given all the words that these apostles must have spoken, and all the things they must have done, these few documents contain only a small portion of the whole. What is truly remarkable is the clarity and the detail of the history recorded by these non-scholars and non-historians.

Acts

Acts begins with Jesus and His apostles in Jerusalem after the resurrection. Jesus spent forty days re-emphasising His teaching about the kingdom of God. He gave a final commission to the apostles, charging them to go into all the world telling His story. He said, 'You are witnesses of these things.' He then ascended into heaven with them looking on.

For the first few chapters of the book, all the action took place in the city of Jerusalem. Although by that time (first century AD) Jews lived in every corner of the world, Jerusalem was still the location of the temple. That meant not only that many Jews lived in Jerusalem, but that Jews from around the world returned several times a year for the feasts prescribed by Moses. On the first major feast after Jesus's ascension, His message was preached. As a result, the word was taken around the world from the very beginning. For when those visiting Jews returned to their distant homes, they no doubt told of the strange happenings in Jerusalem.

Word of Jesus spread, therefore, not just by the apostles, but by common disciples, and even by those who weren't sure what to make of the events and explanations. But regardless of why the message spread, the means of its transmission was always the same: word of mouth.

Of the many radical elements of Jesus's message, one of the most radical was that He meant it to apply to Gentiles (non-Jews), as well as Jews. When Jesus told His apostles to go into all the world, He really meant *all* the world. They thought He meant beyond Jerusalem, but He meant beyond Jews, too. When Gentiles began to show interest in Jesus and His message, the apostles were at first uncertain about what to do. God showed great patience in helping them understand that, indeed, their message was a universal one for all humanity. Towards that end, a man named Saul was called into service.

Saul was the name of the man we call the apostle Paul. He was a Pharisee, very much opposed to the movement that Jesus had started. He persecuted disciples with a vengeance. On the road to Damascus, where he was to harrass them further, however, everything changed. Jesus appeared to him in a brilliant light. Paul was literally knocked off his horse. The experience shook him and reversed the course of his life. Because he was a Pharisee and possessed extensive knowledge of the Scriptures, he became both a disciple and an apostle at the same time.

Instead of being a persecutor, Paul became persecuted. His Hebrew name, 'Saul', became linked with his violent past and was seldom used. Instead, the innumerable souls whom he taught and encouraged called him by his Greek name 'Paul'. The distinction of his particular apostolic ministry was that he was called specifically to bring Jesus's message to the Gentiles. This led to his travelling and teaching throughout the Roman empire.

After Paul encountered the blinding light (Acts 9), we see Peter called to preach to a Roman soldier and his household on the shores of the Mediterranean Sea in a city called Caesarea. When Peter returned to Jerusalem, he was called to account by his Jewish brethren, who wanted to know why he was spreading the message to Gentiles. After some explaining, Peter managed to assure them that this was indeed God's will. Such were the difficulties in birthing a new understanding about Jews and Gentiles.

The last half of the book of *Acts* is concerned with the journeys of Paul. There are a first, second and third missionary journey, followed by a journey to Rome itself. Luke's description of the various cities visited gives an excellent background for understanding the epistles of Paul that follow the book of *Acts*.

Paul developed a strategy for travelling ministry that he followed through all these journeys. Bibles that include maps usually outline Paul's journeys. From these you can see that he generally moved farther westward from Israel with each successive mission. Upon entering a city for the first time, he would look for a synagogue or other place where he could find the Jews of the city located. Remember that in the first century AD, Jews were dispersed throughout the world. There was hardly a city you could enter that didn't have a contingent of Jews who met together regularly. Such meetings usually attracted a number of God-fearing Gentiles as well. With such groups, Paul would begin his preaching and, through those who believed him, reach out to the rest of the city

Sometimes the synagogues were receptive to his message; at other times they were murderously hostile. Most often his remarks divided the local assembly, with some people wanting to hear more of his message and others having heard quite enough. This division befuddled the Roman authorities who couldn't understand why points of Jewish doctrine were so important.

The percentage of Jews who embraced the message of Jesus was probably as great or greater than the percentage of Gentiles who embraced it. But because Jews were such a small percentage of the world's population, the message of Jesus came eventually to be associated with Gentiles more than with Jews. This is ironic when you read the New Testament, which portrays the chief focus of the doctrine (Jesus) and all the major proponents of it (the apostles) as Jewish. This explains why the word 'Christian' appears only twice in the book of *Acts* (and only once elsewhere in the Bible), and why the faith being proclaimed is described by the Roman authorities in *Acts* as a Jewish sect.

Paul stayed longer in some cities than others. Some larger cities, such as Ephesus, became teaching centres through which he could reach outlying areas of the surrounding regions. Paul's goal was to teach his followers well enough that they in turn could teach others. Those who could accept this role were called elders, overseers (from which we derive the word 'bishop') and pastors (another word for 'shepherd'). The two main requirements to serve in these roles were exemplary moral character and the ability to teach. The focus was not on building an organisation, but on getting the word out. For as soon as others could successfully handle the teaching role, Paul was free to move on to another city.

Since many Jews travelled to Jerusalem for some of the annual feasts, and since many apostles were on the road with the message, Paul sometimes found that the Gospel had preceded him to a certain town. This was certainly the case with Rome, the centre of the world in its day. There were many disciples in this metropolis long before Paul reached it.

The book of *Acts* concludes with Paul under house arrest in Rome, but still preaching and teaching about Jesus and the kingdom of God. Thus, the book begins in Jerusalem and ends in Rome, symbolising how Jesus took the faith of ancient Israel and opened it up to the whole world. The open-endedness of the book evokes a sense that the message itself is still going forth. Indeed, the monotheism that ancient Israel clung to in the midst of a polytheistic world has since become a dominant worldview of humanity.

What Remains?

We are now prepared to view the last section of books in the Bible. And having obtained the historical context of Gospels-*Acts*, we are better able to understand their varied purposes and appreciate their common themes.

10

The Apostles' Letters

Having covered all the other continents of Bible literature, we now come to the last: the one we've likened to South America. It is inseparably connected to the Gospels and particularly to the book of *Acts*.

The books in this section are relatively short. Although they are all written in prose, they resemble the books of poetry in that they deal more directly with issues of living. Books of history and prophecy often require the reader to do more work, so far as having to extract principles for living from the text. With the books of poetry and these books, those principles are sometimes closer to the surface.

Letters or Epistles

The last twenty-two books of the Bible are sometimes called letters; at other times epistles. Either term applies. The word 'epistle' helps convey that there was a formal or public element to these letters.

These letters were indeed personal. More often than not, they specify in the text the names of the sender(s) and recipient(s). That makes this section of books the least anonymous of the Bible collection. In most Bible books, the author's persona is buried out of sight. The fact that no point is made of the author's identity implies how unimportant the issue is. With these letters, however, the matter of authorship is central. Since the apostles were charged with the responsibility of spreading Jesus's message faithfully, and since there were false apostles taking advantage of the movement's followers, the apostolic authorship of the letters is what gave them weight with the recipients.

These letters were written to groups of individuals. The disciples in each location would meet for teaching and encouragement. It appears that these letters were written to be read in those assemblies. These assemblies were called synagogues or churches. Both terms refer to the group meeting, but came later to refer also to a particular building set aside for such meetings. Since the letters carried formal instruction, and since they were read to a group, the term 'epistle' is appropriate. Yet that doesn't change the fact that these were letters – simple, written communications. Therefore, either term is fitting.

Practical Correspondence

As we saw in the last chapter, the apostles furthered their movement primarily by word of mouth. They would travel to a city and establish a community of disciples. How long they stayed depended on the needs of that particular community and their desire to spread the message to yet another city. Sometimes they moved on to a new city, only to receive a request for more teaching from the city they had just left. Faced with needing to be in two places at once, the apostles wrote letters to the place they were prevented from visiting.

The imprisonment brought on by persecution gave rise to other letters. If the apostles were incarcerated, they had time on their hands. Writing letters meant they could continue to minister, albeit in a more limited way.

Writing these letters, therefore, was not how the apostles chose to address the church of the future. Though these letters have communicated to the ages, that was not their original purpose. They were a secondary means of linkage, resorted to only when circumstances prevented more direct communication. As with Gospels-*Acts*, these letters are mere shreds and shadows of something far greater that was going on.

If the writers of these letters thought they were writing for a posterity such as you or me, it's not apparent. To put it another way, if they knew their letters were going to be added to and made a part of the Scriptures, they sure didn't act like it. They wrote to specific people in specific locations about specific problems.

Because of the practical nature of these letters, they have some sections which are difficult to understand. For example, Paul in one letter writes, 'Don't you remember that when I was with you, I used to tell you these things?' We who read today want to scream, 'No, Paul, we weren't there; we don't know what "these things" were!'

To make matters worse, there was no postal system in those days. Letters were hand-delivered by apostolic helpers. There was, therefore, no need for a letter to be completely self-explanatory. The helper could elaborate on the writer's location and circumstances, reasons for writing, and general state of mind. Sending a letter by your hand-picked messenger relieves you of having to make the document completely self-sufficient. We who read today, though, don't get the messenger . . . and our understanding suffers to that degree.

Fortunately, much that is in these letters does translate across the ages so that we are only maddened occasionally. If you expect these letters to make perfect sense, as if the apostles were writing directly to you and me, then you are going to be repeatedly frustrated. But if you accept that you and I are being allowed to read ancient correspondence between others, you can gain a great deal from them.

The Letters of Paul

More of the letters are attributed to Paul than to anyone else. His letters come first. They are titled according to their respective recipients. Of course, Paul wrote them without titles – these epistles weren't *that* formal.

Romans

In this letter Paul writes to the disciples in Rome. Normally, he wrote to communities of disciples that he himself had established. *Romans* is an exception, for in this case he wrote in advance of his first visit. By the time this letter was written, the movement had matured considerably. Misunderstandings about the message of Jesus were complex. Paul gives an extended explanation of his understanding of the message. He also deals with the complexities of Jewish versus Gentile perspectives.

Though *Romans* is Paul's longest and perhaps most complex letter, it follows a pattern common for him. That is, the first part of his letter is more theoretical and the last part (that is, starting at Romans 12) more practical. More simply, the first part explains how it is that God loves us, and the second part tells us how we ought to love one another.

1 Corinthians

Corinth was a city in southern Greece. Acts 18 tells how Paul spent eighteen months there. This letter was written sometime after that. Problems had arisen in the group and Paul's help was requested in solving them. Parts of this letter are hard to follow because Paul goes straight into his answers without giving much explanation of each problem. (Remember? He's writing to them, not us. They don't need to be told what their problems are.)

But in 1 Corinthians 13 is the passage about love ('And now these three remain: faith, hope and love. But the greatest of these is love.'). Thus, just when you are about to throw your hands up in despair at this Bible book that is making too little sense, here comes a passage that acts as a psalm for the ages. *1 Corinthians* (and this is true of all the Scriptures) is littered with smaller such diamonds. They can appear when you least expect them.

2 Corinthians

By the time this letter was written, Paul needed to defend himself. Recurring problems at Corinth and the infusion of false teachers had sullied his reputation. This letter is largely a defence of Paul's ministry at Corinth and elsewhere. What makes the letter fascinating is that it doesn't sound defensive! The explanation for this comes near the end of the letter as Paul admits that the purpose of the defence is not to protect his reputation but to defend the truth for those whom he'd taught. It's a wonderfully moving letter. While *Romans* concentrated on the meaning of the message and *1 Corinthians* focused on the application of the message to specific problems, this letter dwells on the motives of the messenger.

The letter also deals with the issue of a collection for the poor in and around Jerusalem. Paul thought it would be a good and welcome gesture for the Gentile disciples to gather a collection to help poor Jewish disciples who were experiencing famine. The people at Corinth were part of that collection. This is another example of how the letters are dovetailed with the book of *Acts*, for it, too, mentions this mission.

Galatians

With *Galatians* begins a sequence of shorter letters. (The first three letters averaged fifteen chapters apiece, while *Galatians* and the five letters that follow it each average less than a third of that.)

Galatia was not a city but a region, situated on the eastern side of Asia Minor. The letter was thus addressed more broadly than the letters to Rome and Corinth. It was intended to be read in various gatherings of disciples in various cities of Galatia. The purpose of the letter was straightforward: to protest and refute false teaching that had taken root in that region.

The more the movement grew and prospered, the more it was plagued by false teaching. Although false teachers were present from the beginning, their numbers and doctrines grew as the movement gained force. After all, parasites have more to gain from a big host than a little one. Although *Galatians* is a letter devoted entirely to the issue, most every other letter makes at least some reference to the problem.

Ephesians

Ephesus was a seaport on the western coast of Asia Minor. In New Testament times this region was called simply Asia. Therefore, whenever you run across the word Asia in the New Testament, *don't* think that it's referring to the continent. Most Bibles use footnotes or some other means to alert readers to the possible confusion.

This letter is very general in nature. Though not as long as *Romans*, it does follow a similar pattern: an explanation of God's design, followed by specific instructions for everyday living. The letter doesn't deal with specific problems, but with general issues of how to be a disciple of Jesus. For this reason the letter may be considered as a circular. That is, it was intended for communities beyond Ephesus as well. *Acts* describes Paul's trips to Ephesus, but there are few specifics in *Ephesians* about those trips.

Philippians

This letter is as personal and specific as *Ephesians* was broad and general. Philippi was a city in northern Greece. Paul preached the message there on his second major journey. The people in Philippi had warm memories of Paul and held him in high esteem. He needed to spend little time defending his ministry to them. Rather, he spends his words in giving them encouragement against the persecution they were facing.

The irony of Paul's encouragement to these people is that it appears he himself was in jail as he wrote this letter. Ever the one to hope, Paul talks of his intent to return to them at some future date. The warmth of the relationship between Paul and these disciples emanates clearly from every line of this short letter.

Colossians

Colossae was a city located due east of Ephesus in Asia Minor. Moreover, this letter is very, very similar to *Ephesians*, except that it is about a third shorter. The structure of the two letters is identical, as are some of the words and phrases. This letter ends with an instruction to send it on to Laodicea, another nearby city. Thus, this also is a kind of circular.

1 Thessalonians

Thessalonica was a city in northern Greece. It was just down the road from Philippi. Paul's first visit there is recorded in Acts 17. As usual, he was met with two contrasting responses: enthusiastic acceptance and vitriolic rejection. Paul's first visit to the city was so brief, he wasn't sure if the acceptance would last. He left behind two of his helpers as he went on to the next city. When those co-workers caught up with Paul, they told him how the disciples in Thessalonica were holding on to their newfound view in the face of continuing persecution.

In response to that report, Paul wrote this letter. It's a letter meant to strengthen and encourage. He emphasises the important points he made while there. Above all, he urges them to look for 'the day of the Lord' when all will be made right.

2 Thessalonians

Sometime after the disciples at Thessalonica got Paul's first letter, they began to wonder about whether 'the day of the Lord' might have come and gone. Paul quickly dashed off this short message to assure them that indeed it hadn't. He urges them to stay with the business of imitating Jesus, loving the people around them with simple and productive lifestyles.

A Slightly Different Kind of Letter from Paul

Up until this point, all Paul's letters have been addressed to communities of disciples. Now we come to the letters addressed to individuals. These individuals were his helpers and co-workers. Nevertheless, it seems likely that these letters were meant to be read in public to the groups that these helpers served. Such a public reading would assure the congregation that the helper was working at Paul's instruction. Therefore, even though these letters bear personal names as titles, the term 'epistle' is still appropriate.

1 Timothy

Timothy was Paul's best known helper. He is first mentioned in Acts 16. Paul met him on one of his journeys, and the two later agreed to work together. Paul writes to Timothy as a father would to a son, so there was a significant age difference between them, as well as a bond of love.

In this letter, Paul's instruction to Timothy revolves around two points. First and foremost, Timothy should continue spreading the message he had learned from Paul. The gist of that message was love, and Paul summed it up this way: '. . . the goal of this command is love, which comes from a pure heart and a good conscience and a sincere faith.' Second, Timothy should appoint others to help spread this message and combat all the false teaching that was springing up everywhere.

2 Timothy

Paul's second letter to Timothy was written when Paul was facing imminent death. Though the Scriptures don't record it, modern historians generally agree that Paul was beheaded in Rome for continuing to preach his message. This letter to Timothy was apparently written in anticipation of that event and is extremely moving.

Paul charges Timothy to continue the good fight of faith. It is the kind of deathbed exhortation you would expect Paul to give: full of concern for others, and no concern at all for himself. He faced death fearlessly and was an example of love to the end.

Titus

Though *Titus* falls after 2 *Timothy* it was obviously written sometime before. It contains none of the immediate anticipation of death. Titus was another helper and co-worker of Paul's.

This letter is structured very much like *1 Timothy*. Paul reminds Titus to give attention to instruction and to the appointment of others who could help spread the message, maintaining and defending the integrity of that message.

Philemon

Philemon takes up barely a page in most Bibles. Though the title is 'Philemon', it's also adressed to Apphia, Archippus and the group of disciples who met in their house. The subject of the letter was a runaway slave of Philemon's named Onesimus. Apparently Paul ran across Onesimus and urged him to return home. At the same time, Paul encourages Philemon not only to forgive Onesimus, but to treat him as a brother rather than a slave.

Paul frequently ended his letters with personal greetings to and from various individuals. Since the list of greetings in this letter is almost identical to the one in *Colossians*, it seems likely that these letters were written at the same time and delivered by the same people. Thus, Philemon probably lived in or near Colossae.

Hebrews

Though the King James version of the Bible attributes this letter to Paul, most modern English versions don't. The uncertainty stems from the fact that if Paul did write this letter, he failed to specify that in the text as he had in all his other letters. Since these letters were hand-delivered, the author was not anonymous to the original recipients – only to us. Regardless of who wrote this epistle, however, it is distinctly different from any of the other letters in the Bible.

This letter leans heavily on quotations from and allusions to Old Testament books. It draws parallel after parallel between previous events recorded in Scripture and contemporary events. The title 'To the Hebrews' is thus an allusion to how the author derived his strategy for living from the history of the Hebrews. He is inviting his readers to join him in identifying with the heroes of Hebrew faith – trusting God in the midst of influences hostile to that faith. All the New Testament books quote and allude to passages from Old Testament books, but *Hebrews* is built almost entirely out of this kind of writing. For this reason, and the fact that it is lengthy, this is a challenging and thought-provoking letter – not to be considered easy reading.

James

This letter is as easy to read as *Hebrews* is difficult. Its language is straightforward, and its subjects are clear. The opening lines indicate that the letter was circulated among various discipling communities. No single destination or group is mentioned. This and the next few letters all derive their titles from the persons who wrote them.

'James' was a common name in New Testament times. This particular James was probably one of the younger brothers of Jesus (he had four of them). *James* gives practical teaching about loving our neighbour and about faith in the middle of trials. It sounds quite similar to the Sermon on the Mount, paraphrasing and reinforcing that great and eloquent message.

1 Peter

This is the first of two letters we have from Peter. It is similar to *James* in several ways. First, it appears to be a circular meant for more than one community. Second, it deals with the same practical subjects of faith, hope and love for everyday living. Third, it's about the same length. Peter's style makes his letter look less like the Sermon on the Mount than James's does. Nevertheless, the underlying principles are the same.

2 Peter

Peter's second letter resembles 2 *Timothy*. The two letters are about the same length, and both are a sort of 'farewell'. Peter begins this letter by pointing out that he does not have long to live and wants to lay down the things most essential for his disciples to remember. While 2 *Timothy* was addressed to an individual, this letter seems to be of the circular variety.

Near the end of this little epistle, Peter makes reference to the fact that he has read some of Paul's letters. He says that there are some things in those letters that are hard to understand. If Peter found some of Paul's writing difficult, you and I should not feel badly if we don't understand them all the first time we read them.

1 John

This is the first of three letters from John. They are sometimes confused with the Gospel of *John*, which bears the same name. The similarity of style between these letters and the inimitable style of the fourth Gospel lead a reader to assume that this is the same John.

This letter is similar to *James* and *1 Peter*. They're all about the same length, are circulated to multiple congregations, and deal with the same practical subjects. What makes the comparision of these three letters so fascinating is how they all manage to make the same basic points with three wildly different styles. Though we have three very different personalities, we come away with the same perspective on God.

2 John

In this very short letter, John deals with the problem of false teachers. He counsels a congregation not to receive visiting teachers who proclaim false teaching. The foundation for this directive is the love he so eloquently wrote about in his first, more general, letter. This letter seems to be addressed to a particular congregation, though his figurative salutation makes the recipient obscure to us.

3 John

Ironically, this letter deals with the flip side of the problem covered in *2 John*. In this case, John writes to a congregation that has been rejecting visiting teachers. Only here, the visiting teacher in question was true, and the leader of the local congregation was wrong to reject. *3 John* and *2 John* are the two shortest books in the entire Bible.

Jude

Jude is only slightly longer than the previous two letters. Jude, like James, was an earthly brother of Jesus. His letter seems to be written at a time when many of the apostles had already been martyred. He makes references to their warnings about false teachers. In *2 Peter*, for example, Peter had warned that false teaching would rise significantly after his passing. Paul had made the same prediction in his farewell in *2 Timothy*. *Jude* makes the point that, indeed, false teaching has now reached those projected proportions. This indicates that the movement had reached a maturity long predicted and anticipated by Jesus and His apostles. Jude's writing thereby sets the stage for the final book of the Bible.

Revelation

The first line of this book reads:

> The revelation of Jesus Christ, which God gave him to show his servants what must soon take place. He made it known by sending his angel to his servant John . . .
>
> Revelation 1:1

From this come the various titles, *The Revelation to John, The Revelation of John* or, simply, *Revelation*. The title is ironic. It proclaims that the book 'reveals', while most readers consider the book almost impossible to understand. Unfortunately, we weren't present when the letter was first written and delivered. We are curious about whether the recipients were as mystified by the contents as we have been.

This is the longest of all the letters. It was addressed to

seven specific communities, all in Asia, and some of which you've heard of: Ephesus, Smyrna, Pergamum, Thyatira, Sardis, Philadelphia and Laodicea. John wrote it from prison on the isle of Patmos, just off the western coast of Asia.

Revelation is much like the book of *Ezekiel*, the last half of *Daniel* and the book of *Zechariah*. Bizarre and conflicting images collide in cataclysmic conflict. This was actually a practised style of writing in those ancient times. It was called 'apocalyptic', and so this book is sometimes called the *Apocalypse* instead of *Revelation*. The meaning is the same because 'apocalypse' comes from a Greek root, while 'revelation' comes from a Latin root.

Like *Hebrews*, this book is built upon quotations and allusions to Old Testament passages. There are hundreds of such references in this letter. To attempt to read this book without first having gained some familiarity with and understanding of the rest of the Scriptures is to invite befuddlement. Even so, the story line is one anyone can appreciate: goodness and evil wage a cataclysmic battle in which goodness wins the decisive victory.

The End or the Beginning?

You've now received a closer look at every one of the Bible's sixty-six books. I hope that from these brief introductions, you will be able to make lifelong friends of at least some of them. To do this, you will discover you need to do more than just read. You will want to understand what you read, and connect it to your own life. To be able to gain the most meaning and value from your Bible reading is what the remaining chapters of this book are all about.

Part Three

The Value of the Bible

11

Reading and Understanding the Bible

The Bible has much to offer readers. To be a reader of the Bible, you have to begin somewhere. You have seen how many places in the Bible there are, besides the beginning, to start reading. When you browse the contents of this huge anthology, you have some sense of its component parts.

Finding a Place to Start: Reviewing the Library's Contents

Figure 11.1 shows the sixty-six volumes of the library in five distinct sections. It is similar to the library shelves you saw in the first chapter, except that the original seven sections (Moses, history, poetry, prophecy, Gospels, *Acts* and letters) have been reduced to five (history, poetry, prophecy, history and letters). I originally cut the pie in seven slices because I thought you'd find it easier to digest that way. But I think you can also see the reasoning behind cutting it five ways, and that adds to your understanding of the Bible's structure.

Perhaps in all this discussion, certain books or sections of books have aroused your interest. If so, those would be a good place to start. Nothing is harder to read than something in which you have no interest; nothing is easier to read than something that has your full attention. On the other hand, you may be equally interested in all of it. In that case, you may want to consider some specific suggestions for starting places.

Psalms makes an excellent beginning place. There are 150 entry points. These entry points vary in length from two verses long to 176 verses long. In other words, there's something for

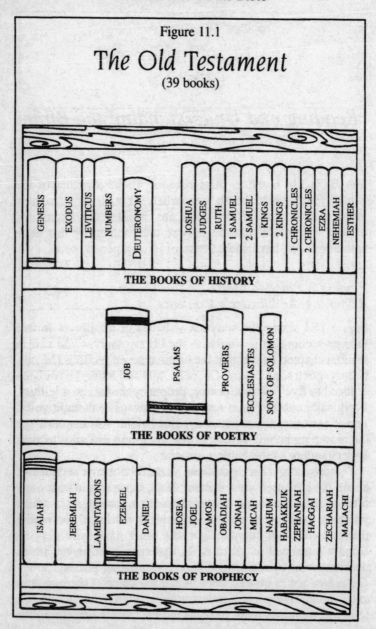

Figure 11.1

The Old Testament
(39 books)

Figure 11.1 (continued)

The New Testament
(27 books)

MATTHEW MARK LUKE JOHN ACTS (of the Apostles)

NEW TESTAMENT HISTORY

ROMANS 1 CORINTHIANS 2 CORINTHIANS GALATIANS EPHESIANS PHILIPPIANS COLOSSIANS 1 THESSALONIANS 2 THESSALONIANS 1 TIMOTHY 2 TIMOTHY TITUS PHILEMON HEBREWS JAMES 1 PETER 2 PETER 1 JOHN 2 JOHN 3 JOHN JUDE REVELATION

LETTERS

every appetite. I'd particularly recommend the twenty-third psalm. From there you can page forwards or backwards, browsing until you find another psalm which appears inviting. If you like Psalm 23, there are certainly others in the collection that will appeal to you.

Proverbs is another excellent place to begin your reading of the Bible. The bites are even smaller, and the themes are simpler, too. Since there are thirty-one chapters, you could decide to read a chapter a day, and you'd have the whole collection finished in a month's time.

Since Jesus is the most striking figure presented in the Bible, reading a Gospel would also be a good logical starting point. There are four to choose from. *Mark* would offer the quickest read, and *John* the most contemplative.

You could always fall back on the idea of reading the Bible

from beginning to end. At least now you'd be prepared to do the skipping and skimming necessary to keep you going through those early books. You would know to skim by the genealogies as you would a page from a phone book, and the tabernacle dimensions as you would an architect's blueprints. And you wouldn't be thrown off course when the eighteenth book starts talking about some man named Job, when you were expecting another extension of the chronological time line in ancient Israel's history.

Pacing Yourself

The Bible has been divided into 1,189 chapters. If you were to set aside five minutes a day to read, you would complete the Bible in slightly over three years. There are all sorts of ways to divide up this elephant so you can eat it one bite at a time. But it's possible you don't want to read the whole Bible. In either case, I've prepared a list (Figure 11.2) which categorises the Bible books according to their length.

The idea behind this list is twofold. First, it allows you to read a whole book in one sitting. Second, it allows you to choose a book based on how long you've got to sit. The three categories are fifteen minutes or less, fifteen minutes to an hour, and longer than an hour. These are approximations for average readers doing a casual reading (not stopping to take notes or study a particular passage in depth). 'Longer than an hour' in most cases means a couple of hours. An evening set aside or a half day off would be more than sufficient for any of them. Since *Psalms* and *Proverbs* are themselves collections, I didn't list them as books to be read whole at one sitting. Rather, you can read any number of their individual parts at one sitting.

Reading Purposes

Various reasons motivate us to read books. We may seek diversion, entertainment, information, or inspiration. Being aware of our purpose makes our reading more effective. In the beginning, your reading of the Bible is likely to be casual.

You're exploring the terrain and want to get a feel for the lie of the land. You won't, therefore, want to be pondering the deep meaning of every other word.

There is, however, enough meat in the Bible that you will probably want to come back and chew over some portions again and again. Unlike a modern mystery, you won't make all the important discoveries in your first reading. Further, there are some portions that you may want to return to just to be able to share them with others. For example, when you run across some of the excellent stories, you might want to read them later to children or grandchildren. For these reasons and others, I encourage you to be prepared to mark in your Bible. Remember that it's a vast country (a world of continents!), and you'll feel more at home as you establish your own landmarks.

Therefore, be willing to dog-ear pages, insert bookmarks, highlight, underline, or draw arrows, or do whatever else helps you find your way back to desirable places . . . or avoid undesirable places! The markings you place in your Bible are the laying of roads in previously uncharted and untravelled territory. Most books don't require this sort of trail-marking, but then most books aren't a collection of numerous writings totalling over a quarter of a million words.

You will probably find great pleasure in exploring the Bible. No, you won't enjoy every page you read, but that won't matter now that you have some idea about what to (at least, initially) pass over. Nevertheless, you'll probably find your greatest pleasure in what you *re-read*. You'll re-read an inspirational passage because you'll know where to find it when you're discouraged. You'll re-read an informational passage because you just couldn't take in all the data the first time around. And you'll re-read a story because all of us like to hear a good story repeated.

The more you re-read the Bible, the more thoughtful, and even meditative, your reading will become. You'll sense when a particular passage invites contemplation. This recognition comes as you find yourself growing in understanding. And the more you grow, the more you find the Bible yielding its treasures to you. The process is so gradual that it's often

Figure 11.2

Books of the Bible

Organised by Time Required for Reading

15 Minutes or Less:

OLD TESTAMENT:

History:
Ruth

Poetry:
any of the Psalms
any of the Proverbs
(or chapters of
the above)

Prophecy:
Joel
Obadiah
Jonah
Micah
Nahum
Habakkuk
Zephaniah
Haggai
Malachi

NEW TESTAMENT:

History:
(none)

Letters:
Galatians
Ephesians
Philippians
Colossians
1 Thessalonians
2 Thessalonians
1 Timothy
2 Timothy
Titus
Philemon
James
1 Peter
2 Peter
1 John
2 John
3 John
Jude

Figure 11.2 (continued)

15 Minutes to an Hour:

OLD TESTAMENT:

History:
Ezra
Nehemiah
Esther

Poetry:
Ecclesiastes
Song of Songs

Prophecy:
Lamentations
Hosea
Amos
Zechariah

NEW TESTAMENT:

History:
(none)

Letters:
Romans
1 Corinthians
2 Corinthians
Hebrews

Longer than an Hour:

OLD TESTAMENT:

History:
Genesis
Exodus
Leviticus
Numbers
Deuteronomy
oshua
Judges
1 Samuel
2 Samuel
1 Kings
2 Kings
1 Chronicles
2 Chronicles

Poetry:
Job

Prophecy:
Isaiah
Jeremiah

NEW TESTAMENT:

History:
Matthew
Mark
Luke
John
Acts

Letters:
Revelation

Ezekiel
Daniel

imperceptible. But you'll find more and more of the Bible making sense. And some pages that at first seem dry as a desert, will all of a sudden have a river of understanding flowing from them. The simple reason for this is that the Bible is a moral book, and the more of its morality you embrace, the more you recognise.

The Bible as a Moral Compass

The Bible presents itself as a moral compass. Its individual writings make constant claims about right and wrong without any equivocation. They are hard to read without feeling that you are being measured by them. A unique experience, maybe? While you're reading a book, you find that it is reading you! Most people who have a high regard for the Bible accept it on its own terms. In other words, they recognise it as a moral book holding forth moral standards. Such people therefore regard the Bible as a legitimate source of moral guidance for life. Perhaps you are not yet prepared to grant it that status. If not, I think it's only a matter of time. For it's hard to continue reading a book which constantly repeats that we should love one another, unless you agree that this represents a legitimate moral code.

I am going to proceed, therefore, on the basis that you desire to move beyond just knowing what the Bible says. You also want to know what it means to us who live today. The conclusions you come to may differ from everyone else's. Because we have individual consciences, this is bound to happen to some degree. Yet to avoid developing moral conclusions, just because others might not see things the same way, is to reject what the Bible presents as its greatest gift: moral understanding.

Moving from What It Says to What It Means

Knowing what the Bible says is the first step to knowing what it means. Yet it is certainly possible to know precisely what the Bible says and totally miss its meaning for us. Fortunately, the Bible itself reveals how this problem occurs and how to avoid it.

As you now know, the Bible was developed over many centuries. In Jesus's day, people were wrestling over the meaning of what had been written in Moses' day. Some of these struggles are recorded for us in the Gospels. Jesus Himself had encountered all the Old Testament books and came up with this one-sentence summation of their meaning:

> ". . . do to others what you would have them do to you, for this sums up the Law and the Prophets."
>
> Matthew 7:12

Jesus is here condensing over 600,000 words into ten. Even *Reader's Digest* doesn't trim that much fat! But there you have it. Too busy to read the Old Testament? Jesus just saved you the trouble. He moved from what it says to what it means.

He phrased it another way on another occasion, but the idea is precisely the same:

> One of them, an expert in the law, tested him with this question: 'Teacher, which is the greatest commandment in the Law?'
>
> Jesus replied, "'LOVE THE LORD YOUR GOD WITH ALL YOUR HEART AND WITH ALL YOUR SOUL AND WITH ALL YOUR MIND.' This is the first and greatest commandment. And the second is like it: 'LOVE YOUR NEIGHBOUR AS YOURSELF.' All the Law and the Prophets, hang on these two commandments.'"
>
> Matthew 22:35–40

The statements in block capitals are direct quotes from the Old Testament. The first is from *Deuteronomy* and the second from *Leviticus*. If you love people, you'll be treating them the way you want them to treat you. Simple.

The apostle Paul paraphrased the Old Testament this way:

> . . . he who loves his fellow-man has fulfilled the law. The
> commandments, 'DO NOT COMMIT ADULTERY,'
> 'DO NOT MURDER,' 'DO NOT STEAL,' 'DO NOT
> COVET,' and whatever other commandment there may
> be, are summed up in this one rule: 'LOVE YOUR
> NEIGHBOUR AS YOURSELF.' Love does no harm
> to its neighbour. Therefore love is the fulfilment of
> the law.

> Romans 13:8–10

The block capital statements in this passage are taken from
the Ten Commandments, which are found in both *Exodus* and
Deuteronomy. Paul comes to the same conclusion as Jesus.

Before Paul was knocked off his high horse, he didn't see the
Bible this way. He was a leading member of a group called the
Pharisees who read the Bible differently. The Pharisees were
largely guilty of hypocrisy in Jesus's day. At one point Jesus
said to them,

> Woe to you, teachers of the law and Pharisees, you
> hypocrites! You give a tenth of your spices – mint,
> dill and cummin. But you have neglected the more
> important matters of the law – justice, mercy and
> faithfulness.

> Matthew 23:23

The Pharisees knew a great deal about what the Bible said,
but were largely ignorant of what it meant. Justice, mercy and
faithfulness are just another way of saying we ought to love
our neighbours or treat them the way we want to be treated.

This last formulation of the fundamental message of the
Scriptures parallels that given by Micah, centuries before
Jesus:

> He has showed you, O man, what is good.
>   And what does the LORD require of you?

> To act justly and to love mercy
> and to walk humbly with your God.
> Micah 6:8

In fact, we have to assume that Jesus was mindful of Micah's words when he spoke of 'justice, mercy, and faithfulness'. His intent was not to depart from the message of the Scriptures, but to bring home the heart of that message.

Noticing How the Bible Interacts with Itself

The Bible frequently interacts with itself. That is, one part of the Bible deals with another. The passages we've just seen do this. Jesus interacts with and interprets the meaning of what Moses said. This gives us an example and head start in doing the same thing. This is another reason why you will want to re-read parts of the Bible. You will see more and more how the thinking of one book informs and leaves an impact on the thinking of others.

For example, you can tell from reading *1 Peter* that he had been reflecting on the meaning of Psalm 34 as he wrote the letter. He even quotes directly from it. Even though you've probably already read Psalm 34, you might want to go back to it, now that Peter's perspective on it has been added to your understanding.

As the Bible writers interact with each other, they keep developing key themes. Because the Bible continually repeats and paraphrases itself, you can be more sure of the things it is driving at. The more an idea is repeated in the Bible, the more important it is. If you've ever raised a child, this is the same way you go about the task of training. Over the course of twenty years, you give out a multitude of different instructions: everything from 'Don't touch!' to 'Be home by midnight.' Running throughout those thousands of instructions, however, are certain recurring themes. We hope our adult children forget the details and live by the themes. And so the Bible does for us.

Because the Bible is an ancient book, and because we receive it in a language foreign to its writers, there are always going to be details of meaning that escape us. There are wordplays in the Hebrew and Greek which never make it into English. But even if you know those ancient languages, little corruptions exist in the text that leave dangling loose ends all over the Bible. So there will always be a sentence here or there that will mystify you and me. A certain word won't make sense. This is why building your understanding of the Bible's message on a verse here or there is so dangerous. If you find one verse saying something that you can't find confirmed by other passages of Scripture, then it's an issue worth dropping. The important ideas are repeated again and again.

People are forever lifting Bible verses out of context and proclaiming, 'The Bible says . . .', and it's some strange thing, entirely contrary to the spirit of the Bible. These sorts of proclamations discourage others from reading the Bible. You have probably had some of your own words quoted exactly, yet taken out of context so that they mean something entirely different from what you intended. If being misinterpreted doesn't invalidate you as a person, it shouldn't invalidate the Bible as a book.

Over the years you may have heard certain Bible verses quoted. Some of these quotes may have puzzled or troubled you. You are now in a position to look up those quotes in context, and see if the context sheds light that drives away your confusion. Often you will find just such light. You will be developing your own understanding of the Bible, instead of being entirely dependent upon someone else's explanation of it.

In the United States, where I live, both primary political parties invoke the memory of Abraham Lincoln and quote his words. Does this mean it's a waste of time to study Lincoln's life, or that his ideas are so confusing that they can be used to support two contrary political agendas? No. It means that only those who make the effort to know something about Lincoln are in a position to decide which current political direction is more faithful to his thinking. Such people are not entirely dependent on some 'expert' for their understanding of Lincoln.

The more you read the Bible, the more you'll notice how

it interacts with itself. And the more you notice that, the more you'll feel comfortable interacting with it yourself. The simplest interplay to notice is when a New Testament book quotes an Old Testament book. Many Bibles take pains to make such quotes noticeable. Beyond these, however, are many more subtle interactions. You don't see too many among the New Testament books because these writings were produced during the same generation in a wide variety of locations. The writer of a given New Testament book had little access to the rest of the New Testament writings. But in the Old Testament, where the writings were accumulated over many generations, you'll find a writer often alluding to previous writings. Some of these allusions are subtle and only become apparent after many readings.

Noticing How the Bible
Deals with Changing Circumstances

The Bible's writers understood full well the difficulties of the lives we lead here on earth. They were not eternal optimists and they knew nothing of rose-coloured spectacles. The Bible is a reality-based book. Being moral, or doing right, requires thought, for it's not always easy to know what to do. Jesus Himself sweated blood the night before He died, as He made decisions about His final course of action.

While presenting the notion of unchanging truth emanating from a Creator God, the Bible also acknowledges that different circumstances call for different behaviour. In fact, behaviour that is commended in one part of the Bible may be condemned in another. The reason for this is not a changing moral standard. Rather, it is that the Bible is constantly looking beyond the behaviour to the spirit that drives it. That is, the Bible is even more concerned with the motives for our behaviour than for the behaviour itself.

Paul points this out in the beginning of his great treatise on love (*the* theme of the Scriptures) in 1 Corinthians 13:

> If I speak in the tongues of men and of angels, but
> have not love, I am only a resounding gong or a
> clanging cymbal. If I have the gift of prophecy and
> can fathom all mysteries and all knowledge, and if I
> have a faith that can move mountains, but have not
> love, I am nothing. If I give all I possess to the poor
> and surrender my body to the flames, but have not
> love, I gain nothing.
>
> 1 Corinthians 13:1–3

Paul lists activities that almost anyone would consider 'good deeds'. Yet without love as their motive, they amount to nothing. In some cases, they amount to less than nothing ('resounding gongs' and 'clanging cymbals'). Paul came to learn this importance of motive the hard way. As a Pharisee, he was extremely zealous about keeping the Sabbath holy. This meant copying the behaviour of Nehemiah, who once threatened force against those who would break the Sabbath. Nehemiah was justified in his behaviour because he was genuinely concerned for the glory of God and the well-being of his nation. The Pharisees, however, were motivated more selfishly and self-righteously, and thus were condemned for doing the same thing Nehemiah did. Their motive was radically different from his.

Similarly, Moses included in the law a provision for stoning those caught in adultery. Jesus had the same revulsion over adultery that Moses did, but He wouldn't stone an adulteress brought to Him. For one thing, where was the man? For another, the situation was entirely different. Moses was trying to establish a moral nation; Jesus was trying to teach individuals how to live morally in the middle of an immoral nation. The principles and motives of these two teachers were precisely the same, but the circumstances they faced were very different.

I have not always found it easy to determine how changing circumstances affect principles taught in the Bible. But it is easy to recognise that practising Moses' law in our day is impractical and undesirable. In the first place, most of us aren't physical descendants of Abraham, and that's who Moses' words addressed. Second, even today's physical descendants of Abraham can't practise the rituals Moses prescribed, because there's no tabernacle in which to sacrifice the animals. Besides, who finds it meaningful to sacrifice animals these days anyway?

The Bible over and over shows itself willing to let the externals pass away while clinging to principles. When David planned the temple, he extracted principles from Moses' tabernacle. But he did not rebuild the same tent-like temporary structure. And by the time the temple was destroyed in 70 AD, Jesus had already shown that we ought to be treating the whole earth – not just one particular building – as God's temple.

Deciding what is a principle that stays and what is a particular that passes away is a job for our consciences. As human beings, you and I are each equipped with a conscience. Whatever moral understanding we receive from the Bible must be processed through this conscience for it to be of any use to us. To do something the Bible says which violates our own conscience is not something the Bible asks of us. The Bible isn't a substitute for the conscience; it's a nourishment to conscience.

Moral Sense Is Built Upon Common Sense

An unnecessary question often arises when people consider reading the Bible. They ask, 'Do I take the Bible literally?' Indeed, there are people who profess to take the Bible literally, and there are also people who profess that they could never take it literally. But neither of these two groups takes a reasonable position. They are being unreasonable, because what book (much less collection of books) speaks either entirely literally or entirely without being literal? Most books, indeed most people, speak with a combination of both literal and figurative expressions.

Has someone ever told you that it was raining 'cats and dogs'? If so, did you take them literally? The internal thinking mechanisms by which we make all the little decisions necessary to decide whether someone is using a figure of speech are intricate and vast. But we sum up the process by calling it 'common sense'. You must apply common sense when you are reading the Bible. If Jesus calls Himself the good shepherd, you must decide whether He means He's resigning the ministry in order to take up sheepherding, or whether He is speaking figuratively of His leadership role.

Using common sense doesn't guarantee that you'll always understand everything you read in the Bible. But disregarding common sense will guarantee that you misunderstand quite a bit of it. After close to two decades of reading the Bible daily, I can say this: when I read the Bible, I sometimes understand parts of it. This has been true from the beginning. What has changed is that I understand more parts of it with each passing year. I have found that the key to finding value in the Bible is not taking it literally, but taking it seriously.

Taking the Bible seriously means avoiding mysticism on the one hand, and scepticism on the other. Some people get so mystical about the Bible that they obscure its practical side. After all, it is just a book. Giving it enormous lip service without applying your best critical reasoning to it amounts only to bibliolatry – the idolatry of a book. Ironically, idolatry is a practice the Bible continually condemns. On the other hand, being sceptical about everything you read in the Bible is unwarranted. Such scepticism is evidence of prejudice and a closed mind. No book, ancient or modern, would survive the jaundiced eye that some bring to the Bible.

The Bible can be approached as we would approach any book. As with any book, its peculiarities have to be considered. I have described the Bible's peculiarities: its size, eclectic composition, ancient origin, and so on. Combine this information with your common sense, and, whenever you read the Bible, you'll be able to understand parts of it.

Read with a View to Do

One of the greatest hindrances to understanding the Bible is failing to put into practice those moral principles that we recognise in it. This, Jesus pointed out, was the problem with the hypocritical Pharisees who criticised Him. They had false understandings of the Bible because they applied its judgments to other people, rather than themselves. In other words, they professed an allegiance to the Scriptures but used its standards to judge others, rather than to judge their own lives. They did not practise what they preached.

It is one hazard of being a human being, that we expect others to live up to standards which we ourselves don't maintain. The gist of 'doing justice and showing mercy' is holding ourselves to high ethical standards and making allowances for others. In terms of road safety they call this attitude 'defensive driving'. They say that to avoid accidents, obey all the traffic laws yourself, but make allowances for others who won't. The reason we have so many 'accidents' in the course of daily living is that we are understanding about our own shortcomings but can't figure out why everyone else is not doing what they're supposed to.

What I am saying is that the life you live away from the Bible has something to do with how much you understand when you're reading the Bible. Anyone who tries to live a moral life knows how difficult it is to live up to one's own standards – much less anyone else's. Our failures at perfection can produce in us self-justifying denial of our shortcomings at one extreme, or demoralised abandonment of a moral lifestyle at the other. Midway between these two extremes is a humble admission that our moral standards are still within sight . . . but not yet within reach. Such an attitude finds the spirit of the Bible, because this is the sense from which it was written.

There are many facets of the Bible that can be appreciated simply with observation: its lyrical high notes, its dignity of presentation, its resilience over time, and so on. But its greatest treasure – insight into the unseen moral dimensions of life – is reserved for those who are not content to merely observe. They must live out their level of moral understanding. As they do, they find that return trips to the Bible increase that level of understanding.

On Your Own

With many of the issues that face us, we can't just open up the
Bible and turn to a page that says, Rule Number 547: 'Do this',
or Rule Number 548: 'Do that'. You will simply not find in it
such clear-cut directives for most of the moral questions you
will encounter. We can become so wearied by the questions of
life that we wish the Bible would come right out and magically
say, 'Here's what you should do.' Alas, this is not the role it
has carved out for itself.

The Bible is a compendium of moral thoughts designed to
nourish moral minds. At least that's my view on it. You may,
especially as you read it more and more, see things differently.
That's one of the glories of the Bible: it's free to speak for itself.
And you can read it for yourself. I hope that I have equipped
you – and inspired you – to do just that.

About the Author

Michael Gantt was born in 1951 in Columbia, South Carolina. In 1979 he left a business career and moved to St Louis, Missouri, where he studied and taught the Bible – mainly as a pastor – for fifteen years. He has earned both a Master of Divinity degree and a Doctor of Ministry degree. He has now returned to business and to South Carolina where he is an executive with Policy Management Systems Corporation. He and his wife Janie are the parents of four children.

NIV Thematic Study Bible
General Editor: Alister McGrath

The best commentary on Scripture is Scripture itself:

'I am an enthusiast for the NIV Thematic Study Bible . . . because its maxim of letting Scripture explain Scripture is so completely right-minded . . .'

J I Packer

Using the *NIV Thematic Study Bible*, readers can:
* identify and explore the leading themes of Scripture
* see how themes interweave and develop through the Bible
* come into direct contact with and rapidly access the relevant Scriptures with the minimum of subjective comment

The *NIV Thematic Study Bible* has many unique features:
* over 120,000 theme references appear, over half of them in the margins of the Bible pages. These indicate the key themes of the Bible text and refer the reader to the Thematic Section of the Bible for detailed study

* over 2,000 themes appear in the Thematic Section. These include:
   > an explanation of each theme
   > key Bible references on the theme
   > cross references to related themes

* Themes are arranged in a nine-fold classification system based on Scripture:

God	Creation	God's people
Jesus Christ	Humanity	The life of the believer
Holy Spirit	Sin and Salvation	Last things

* introductions to each book of the Bible, emphasising each book's themes
* almost 200 panels giving more detailed descriptions of key themes
* an alphabetical index of themes, panels and book introductions
* colour maps

Cased, blue	ISBN 0 340 56708 2
Calfskin, black	ISBN 0 340 65660 3